Teaching Empathy

A Blueprint for Caring, Compassion, and Community

David A. Levine

Solution Tree | Press

a division of

Solution Tree

555 North Morton Street
Bloomington, IN 47404
800.733.6786 (toll free) / 812.336.7700
FAX: 812.336.7790

FSC
Mixed Sources
Product group from well-managed
forests and other controlled sources
Cert no. SW-COC-002283
www.fsc.org
© 1996 Forest Stewardship Council

email: info@solution-tree.com
solution-tree.com

Printed in the United States of America

ISBN 978-1-935249-00-9

Dedication

For my three loves:

Gideon,

Sam,

and

Jodi

In memory of my fiddle teacher:
Tim Ryan (1948–2005)

*Timmie not only taught me
about music but about life
through the soulful gentleness
with which he lived his.*

Table of Contents

Acknowledgments

As I have journeyed the road of my professional life, I have met and learned from many amazing, talented, and caring people. I will always be grateful to Val Mihic who is one of the deepest and most thoughtful teachers I have had the pleasure of working with. Many of the thoughts conveyed in these pages grew out of conversations in a car as we traveled back and forth to Amenia, New York, in 2001 and 2002. Bill Plotkin is a man of imagination, passion, courage, and wisdom. I shall always be grateful to him for helping me find my voice of heart expression. Bob Barrette has consistently listened over the last 20 years and continues to encourage and watch out for me. He also was most gracious in allowing me to share his story of Mrs. Arns. Jerry Kreitzer is a rare human being. I am honored to call him a colleague and friend. Ricia McMahon, through her caring ways, has shown me how to synthesize my own experiences into lessons for others. Tom Turney continues to be a wise and gifted presence in my life. I am grateful to call him a friend. Jim Lew provided me with my first in-service learning experience in the second week of my teaching career. He quickly became a friend and mentor, helping me shape my beliefs regarding school culture and its relationship to healthy learning.

Tom Connelly mentored me in the idea of creating a "protective factors culture" for students in schools. He also provided me with the freedom to craft numerous learning opportunities for his colleagues in the Wappingers Falls Central School District. Tom Maletto, Laura Sagan, Marvin Kreps, Mary Anne Domico, Robert Katulak, Ileana Eckert, Debra Hogencamp, and Terry Kenney all invited me to work with their students and colleagues, never once hesitating in their support, showing the belief that helped me develop much of the work in this book. Special thanks to Susan Striepling, Art Costa, Eileen Hurst, Daniel Goleman, James Garbarino, and all who have read my manuscript and provided valuable feedback.

Thanks to the team at Solution Tree (formerly National Educational Service), to president Jeff Jones, Suzanne Kraszewski, Rhonda Rieseberg, Amanda Samulak, Elisabeth Wieser, and Amy Shock, all of whom were so responsive, patient, and open to my ideas and questions as we moved along with this project. A special thanks to Jeff for getting the process going and for believing in my work. Suzanne in particular supported this book from the beginning and provided me with its first critique, launching me on my way. Thanks also to Julia Copeland who helped me with some of the earliest writing. A special thanks goes to my editor Larry Liggett, who lived with this manuscript for 3 months and was so supportive, enthusiastic, and skillful in helping craft this book into its completed form.

As for the music used in the mini-curriculum on empathy in section 4, as a child, I often fell asleep to the sounds of my parents singing traditional folk songs: thanks Mom and Dad. Jay Ungar and Molly Mason have been a constant source of inspiration, friendship, and encouragement. Their music is a gift to the world, and I have felt honored to play with them through the years. I am equally grateful to my fellow musical travelers who played on the CD: Fooch Fischetti, John Parker, and especially to my bandmates Debbie Lan, John P. Hughes, and Dean Jones. Dean is a musical wizard and phenomenal producer whose creativity, passion, talent, and enthusiasm helped make the music what it is. Thanks to Sam Levine, Jodi Palinkas, and Chris Andersen for coaching me through the recitations.

I am forever grateful to the staff and students in the schools I have the privilege of working in every day, especially in the following school districts: North Rockland, Rhinebeck, Webutuck, New Paltz, Clarkstown, Poughkeepsie, Garrison, and Pearl River in New York state, and in New Jersey, Evesham, Jackson, and Lower Cape May.

I thank David Whyte who inspired many of the frameworks presented in this book through his poems, prose, and workshops. Thanks to songwriter and educator Bob Blue for his powerful and thought-provoking song "Courage."

Finally, I want to thank songwriter Lee Domann whose moving song "Howard Gray" has guided me toward so much of the work I do in schools. I consider him to be a gifted songwriter and a life-long friend.

About the Author

David A. Levine is a teacher, author, and musician who has been working with school systems across the United States and abroad since 1984. Using music to enter into dialogue with teachers and students, he seeks to facilitate the creation of emotionally safe schools where all people have a sense of place and purpose.

Levine was previously the chief trainer for the Northeast Regional Center's Safe and Drug Free Schools Program for the United States Department of Education. He has also taught elementary and middle school and has offered training sessions, institutes, and keynote speeches for hundreds of school districts, state agencies, and other educational organizations across the country.

Levine is the author of *Building Classroom Communities: Strategies for Developing a Culture of Caring.* He also co-produced the bullying-prevention music video-documentary *Through the Eyes of Howard Gray,* an honorable mention at the Columbus Video and Film Festival in the education category. His musical CD, *Dance of a Child's Dreams* (Angel Records), received the Parent's Choice Gold Award for children's music, and his articles have appeared in the journals *Educational Leadership, Reclaiming Children and Youth,* and *School Safety.* He lives with his family in New York's Hudson River Valley.

If you are interested in enhancing the implementation of the ideas from *Teaching Empathy* into your school, David A. Levine is available to work directly with your teachers and students, providing an in-depth approach to creating an emotionally safe learning community. This 2-day offering trains teachers in how to apply the various approaches presented in *Teaching Empathy* and includes the introduction of many of the songs on the CD to the students in a workshop/dialogue format.

Introduction

Little Steps, Long Journey

Two roads diverged in a wood, and I—
I took the one less traveled by,
And that has made all the difference.

—"The Road Not Taken," Robert Frost (1920)

I have always loved the poem "The Road Not Taken" because it is a reminder that we all face choices in life and that sometimes the best choice is not the easiest one to make. The finest choice leads to multiple opportunities for even more choices, and opportunity for positive change—a chance to reach that place of happiness and contentment where most of us want to be. It all starts with the energy of our initial steps forward. Energy, in this sense, is movement that comes from strong emotions. Young people possess a great deal of this energy, and we can help them use this reservoir in positive ways as they face life's many challenges.

This is a book about teaching that we all have choices in each moment we share with others. These choices include empathy, compassion, caring, and generosity. At first glance, these choices seem so natural and basic, but in fact they are often missing within relationships in school. Teaching empathy combines the many dynamics of human interactions such as honoring and not judging others, acting in caring and compassionate ways, and respecting the other person by focusing and listening to him or her.

There is a story told by Robert Fulghum in his book *All I Really Need to Know I Learned in Kindergarten* (1988) about a youth group he was working with. On one occasion, Fulghum instructed some 80 children to decide whether they were giants, wizards, or dwarves for a game on forming groups. As Fulghum watched these young people scampering about laughing, screaming, and having a good time with each other, he suddenly felt one little girl tug on his pants leg. He looked down at her and she asked, "Where do the mermaids stand?" Fulghum, in a moment of intuitive brilliance, responded, "The mermaid stands right by the King of the Sea." At this point, he took hold of the little girl's hand and there the two of them stood, watching the mad scene of giants, wizards, and dwarves (pp. 83-85).

Fulghum's response indicated his presence in the moment with that little girl and, more importantly, his presence with his own internal compass that guided him toward the direction of the little girl's needs. Every day in schools there are millions of students who in some way are asking, "Where do I stand?" Often, students do not ask this question as clearly as the little girl in Fulghum's story. Instead, these young people are often in need of belonging and acceptance. They are in search of a caring teacher who will invite them into a circle of belonging and acceptance, a teacher who will place them into a ring of safety and offer a firm hand of guidance as the students learn the skills necessary to explore their lives in the future and succeed.

Teaching Empathy reflects the influence of many life experiences I have had professionally as an educator and personally in my relationships with others—including my own children—in my quest to respond to life's many challenges. Empathy as a guiding principle of life is the core dynamic for emotionally satisfying relationships. By its very nature, empathy also serves as a wellspring of optimism and hope, providing new ways of seeing and reawakened ways of imagining with an awareness of the potential of each moment we share with others.

This book focuses on teaching the pro-social skill of empathy by naming and practicing it, and by modeling and encouraging empathy. It is a book about building a culture of caring in school through empathic acts and by making school a place where each student feels emotionally safe and can see, by example, that a life's journey is composed of single steps and that he or she can influence the shape of that journey by the small choices made every day.

Teaching Empathy is divided into four sections. Section 1 focuses on how teachers must model empathy and other compassionate behaviors as a primary approach to teaching pro-social skills and building trusting relationships. Section 2 presents specific ways of teaching students the skill of empathy and its companion behaviors: listening, compassion, honor, and generosity. Section 3 highlights strategies for building the empathic culture of a school through what I call the intentions of the school of belonging. Section 4 is a mini-empathy skill-building curriculum that applies many of the ideas, approaches, and processes presented in the first three sections.

A significant part of section 4 is a CD of songs and recitations. I have utilized the universal language of music as a teacher since my career began. The CD in this resource is the result of thousands of successful lessons. I call the process I present in the curriculum Music/Dialogue (MD). The MD process has helped me facilitate many meaningful and memorable social skills lessons. The enclosed CD and the lessons in section 4 will help you do the same with your students.

By its very nature, empathy is difficult to teach because it straddles the line between cognition (rational thought) and emotion (which is not always rational or easily managed). Empathy as a skill is a multifaceted process that moves along a continuum from observation to thought and finally to feeling and action. Each step must be given its due share of focus in order for the empathy skill to be as natural as when someone says, "excuse me," "thank you," "you're welcome," "hello" and "goodbye." These are examples of social skills that are learned by children early in life as expected ways of responding, as habits when interacting with others. It is imperative that educators find emotionally meaningful ways for students to channel their observations and reflections of social situations (thoughts) to caring and compassionate acts (empathy skills). *Teaching Empathy* has been designed to provide the strategies and processes for doing just that.

Section 1

Teaching Empathically: When Teachers Make Connections

*May the beauty we love
be what we do.*

—Jelaluddin Rumi, Persian Poet

The Reasons for Teaching Empathy

In 1951, Bob's family moved to a new neighborhood in his home city of Niagara Falls, New York. He was in third grade at the time and his new teacher was not particularly friendly or helpful. He almost failed. By fourth grade, Bob did not like school: it wasn't much fun and he had discovered that the one way he could gain attention was by being the class clown. One day in early October, his teacher Mrs. Arns surprised Bob when she said, "I've been noticing what nice handwriting you have. We're having a class handwriting contest in a couple of weeks. You should enter." That's all Bob needed to hear. Over the next 2 weeks, he practiced his "Palmer Method" handwriting technique every chance he had. Bob won the class contest and went on to win the school-wide contest as well. His handwriting paper and photo appeared in the awards case in the school lobby. This achievement is something Bob still remembers with pride. One day Mrs. Arns gave him a book about a character named Kit Carson and suggested he might like it. He liked it so much that he read it in one night—all 131 pages of it. The next day when Mrs. Arns asked Bob if he had started the book, he told her not only had he had started it but he had finished it, too. She told the entire class about his accomplishment.

When Bob entered fifth grade, his teacher told him that Mrs. Arns had said what a good student he was, particularly in history. Years later, in his first year as a history teacher in the same Niagara Falls school district, Bob sought out Mrs. Arns, who was still teaching. "I won a handwriting contest when I was in your fourth-grade class," he said. "Sit down, young man," Mrs. Arns said. They sat down and Mrs. Arns continued. "I want you to know that was the only handwriting contest we ever had in our school." She had created it specifically for Bob.

Bob's story is also the story of a teacher who practiced empathy as she made caring connections with her students. In order for our students to feel cared for and motivated, we need to intentionally create connecting environments. A connecting environment is nonjudgmental and emotionally safe: a place where the unique story held within each child's heart is given voice through listening and responsiveness, where each child and his or her story is accepted and honored. When a teacher practices empathy and concentrated focus on the child, each student behavior is seen for what it is: as a form of communication reflecting what needs are met or unmet. When identified in this way, these needs provide a symbolic road map for understanding what helpful path that teacher needs to take. Bob's roadmap pointed Mrs. Arns in the direction of giving him a reachable goal with an opportunity to succeed and shine.

When a teacher demonstrates love for her work, is consistent and predictable, and is able to see that *little things are truly big things*, she can have a tremendous impact on the future of that child far more than any test score ever will. In this case, not only did Bob become a teacher, but he also became a husband, father of four, a stalwart member of his community, and my friend. He befriended me during my first harried year of teaching (I had his son Greg in my fourth-grade class), and helped steer me in the direction of what I am doing today—working toward the creation of emotionally safe learning environments.

I have been facilitating human relations workshops for faculty, staff, and students in schools since 1984. I often hear concerns from teachers that students are not nice to each other, that they put each other down, and that they can be mean and cruel. The message "Be nice to others" is not a new concept for students, and it is often met with looks of "Oh, this again" upon delivery. Herein lies our greatest challenge: How can we teach empathy, compassion, caring, and generosity in relevant, meaningful, and memorable ways?

Empathy education is one of the most critical educational issues of our time because it is only when students feel emotionally safe and secure in all areas of the school environment—in the classroom, hallway, or cafeteria; at recess; and on the bus—that they will begin to focus and tap into the unlimited potential that lies within each of them.

Consider how emotionally safe a student might feel after one of the following exchanges:

Teacher: *Did you study?*

Student: *Yes, I did.*

Teacher (with sarcasm): *Oh, I bet.*

Student: *I'm having surgery on my leg this weekend, and I'll be out for 2 weeks. Could you give me the work that I'll miss while I'm out?*

Teacher: *That's not my problem.*

In these examples, the teacher behaved the same way. These stories were shared by parents with other participants during an evening workshop I was facilitating on bullying in school. In each case, the teacher is the one doing the bullying, and it is an antisocial *teacher* behavior that has no place in school just as the antisocial behaviors of students have no place in school. Linda

Darling-Hammond, a professor of teaching and teacher education at Stanford University, was quoted in the *New York Times* (1996) as saying, "Everyone knows that bullying of students by teachers exists, but the treatment of kids by teachers in the classroom is rarely discussed." Daniel Olweus, the preeminent researcher on the topic of bullying, found that "2 percent of the 2,400 students questioned had been bullied by teachers." Olweus also calculated that "a surprising number of teachers, an estimated 10 percent, had engaged in verbal harassment, or bullying of students" (as quoted in Marano, 1996).

Negative school experiences that continue over time can beat a student's sense of hope down to the point where the student's outlook on school and life becomes bleak and tiresome rather than what it should be: *alive and spirited.* We know from experience—our own and the experiences of our children and students—that a strong emotional experience for a child becomes an imprinted moment that lives forever within the child's psyche. For example, many adults have vivid memories of being lost or separated from their parents or caregivers when they were children. Perhaps the incident occurred in a department store or in an amusement area, but the frightening experience of separation is so strong that it remains imprinted upon the adults. Although the event happened many years ago, they can remember where the incident took place, the feelings they had, what they were wearing, who helped them, and so on. While describing such memories, the physical sensations of the incident that happened long ago return to the person sharing them and are eerily familiar. Whether or not they are conscious of it, the adults are recalling an emotionally coded event—an experience that continues to affect them throughout their lives.

Fortunately, it is not only negative experiences, such as being lost long ago, that can become emotionally coded. Positive experiences can also be imprinted in this way—even the positive experiences of a response to a teacher who shows an interest and who truly cares. In this age of standards and high-stakes testing, the level of connection a student feels toward his or her school and the adults who work and teach there is as critical a standard as there is. The answers to the following questions will provide a revealing gauge of how connected your students feel to their school:

- Do your students enjoy being at school?
- Do they feel that students are nice to each other?
- Do they feel that their teachers like them?
- Are their emotions impacted memorably in healthy and positive ways?
- Are their relations with others healthy and positive?

There is nothing more painful and discouraging than feeling alienated and alone, especially in school where relationships are paramount. If this feeling of alienation and aloneness becomes a pattern, it then becomes a way of life. The purpose of school is for students to learn academically, socially, and emotionally to their fullest potential. This will not happen if they feel unconnected to the experiences and the people around them, especially their teachers.

When the National Longitudinal Study of Adolescent Health (Add Health, n.d.) was begun in 1994 as the "largest, most comprehensive survey of adolescents ever undertaken," its purpose was to "determine the causes of health-related behaviors of students in grades 7–12 and to follow-up and re-interview the participants in young adulthood to investigate the influence that adolescence has on adulthood" (www.cpc.unc.edu/projects/addhealth).

The following excerpt is from a monograph based on the first analysis of Add Health data. The monograph, *Protecting Adolescents From Harm: Findings From the National Longitudinal Study on Adolescent Health*, was initially published in the September 10, 1997, issue of *JAMA, The Journal of the American Medical Association* (Resnick et al., 1997).

> *The school environment also makes a difference in the lives of youth, but not in the conventional ways we often think of schools. School policies, classroom sizes, and teacher training appear unrelated to the emotional health and behaviors of students. Instead, what matters is the students' sense of connection to the school they attend: if students feel they are a part of the school, are treated fairly by teachers, and feel close to people at school, they have better emotional health and lower levels of involvement in risky behavior. Feeling that other students are not prejudiced is also protective for students in some cases. Future analyses of Add Health data can explore why some students feel connected to their schools while others do not, and how schools can better create a sense of connectedness among their students.* (p. 32)

Teachers must seek to cultivate caring relationships with their students by seeing them as the unfinished works of art that they are, with emotional needs that must be met, nourished, and satisfied. When an emotional need is unmet, the young person's behavior will reflect it, and often such behavior is considered antisocial because the negative behavior is displayed or directed at others—in a sense, the child is taking his or her anger, frustration, or fear out on others or even on the school. Any child who is a victim of the subtle forms of bullying that happen in most schools every day—things such as teasing, put-downs, name calling, or sarcasm—will come to see the school experience as a hostile one (Hoover & Olsen, 2001, p. 14). These low-level forms of aggression are considered subtle because they often go unnoticed. For example, I am referring to such things as negative comments said under one's breath to another student during class or intentionally excluding someone from a group, forcing him or her to sit alone or at the "fringe" table with the other loners in the cafeteria.

Certainly, educators must be concerned with stopping student behaviors such as bullying, harassment, and exclusion, but the primary concern educators must address is how to change the conditions of intolerance in school that cause students to act antisocially in the first place. When teachers allow intolerance by students toward one another to exist, they are planting the seeds of alienation. Low-level forms of aggressive behavior must not be accepted; instead, replacement behaviors or choices must be modeled and taught. We must teach young people about practicing empathy, honoring others, and offering support to their peers by offering support ourselves and providing our students with opportunities to express their feelings through words and actions.

Seeing Things Differently

There is no educational issue more important than shaping student behavior positively in an atmosphere void of intolerance

from others. If a teacher identifies intolerance solely as a diction-
ary would define it—as prejudice, bias, bigotry, chauvinism, par-
tiality, racism, and sexism—then the task of integrating tolerance
education into the classroom experience could feel overwhelming
and potentially controversial. This could cause some teachers to
stay away from dealing with the tolerance issue altogether.

My friend Jim Lew facilitates diversity workshops in the cor-
porate world. He has told me that people resist the idea of a
diversity workshop when they have either had a negative experience or have heard about negative experiences others have
endured. Jim often hears statements such as, "Hey, we had a
diversity training here with our employees a number of years
ago, and it was the worst experience we ever had. We're still
recovering from that one." Jim points out that diversity does not
only deal with race or gender issues; these are the "hot" issues
that can create separation and defensiveness within a group. It
is often hard to get past this dynamic during a learning situation
when people may already be feeling vulnerable. Diversity really
means the different ways people see the world. We all have
screens, or filters, that information or data pass through. These
screens are like eyeglasses; the prescriptions for our individual
eyeglasses are based on all of our life experiences. Once information passes through our unique screens, it becomes our perceived reality. If that perception is not analyzed or challenged, it
can be viewed as fact. To illustrate this point, Jim will show the
following phrase to a group:

FEATURE FILMS ARE THE RE-
SULT OF YEARS OF SCIENTIF-
IC STUDY COMBINED WITH
THE EXPERIENCE OF YEARS.

He then asks people in the group to individually count up the number of "Fs" in the phrase. Some see three, others four, and so on up to six (the actual number). After some laughter and banter throughout the audience, Jim will show how the "F" in the word "OF" is often missed because it sounds like a "V." Also the "F" in "SCIENTIFIC" is often overlooked because it comes at the end of a line and the eye has already scanned to the beginning of the next line.

After reviewing this phrase together as a group, all participants are able to see the same number of "Fs." The point is that most times when people have a different point of view, they take a defensive posture for protection and control rather than a collaborative posture that leads to understanding and unity. Collaboration often comes through collective exploration. Even if group members initially have differing viewpoints, if each person holds the intention for group success through listening, reflection, and exploration of ideas instead of working from *perceived* reality and assumptions, then the group process more often than not will lead to bonding, appreciation, group cohesiveness, and success.

Jim's metaphorical exercise underscores the importance of "seek[ing] first to understand then to be understood" (Covey, 1989, p. 235). Covey's advice is vital for any teacher—in fact, it should become *habit.* In order to instill in our students the importance of accepting and helping all people, we must model these traits ourselves. Each child has his or her perceived reality, and unless we empathize with each child to understand what that perceived reality is, we will find ourselves reacting to the child's behaviors with frustration and anger rather than responding to him or her with compassion and understanding.

When we respond to a behavior in an effort to understand it, we also gain a greater ability to shape it in a positive way.

I recently worked with a seventh-grade teacher who shared the following story. One day a group of girls in her class came to school wearing their jeans inside out. The students were called down to the office by the assistant principal. After they returned to class, this teacher, out of amused curiosity, asked why they were wearing their jeans that way. The girls responded, "We do it because it makes the assistant principal mad." I am sure they enjoyed controlling the behavior of the assistant principal who, in their minds, was always trying to control their behavior. The teacher telling me this story identified the larger issue in this situation: the girls and some teachers believed that because this group of students was often in "trouble" with the assistant principal, he had "profiled" them as the bad kids. This private logic of the administrator certainly did not indicate an emotionally safe school for the students in the group, and their behavior reflected this.

There is always more to a person than is initially evident. When people do not seek to learn everything they can about someone before accepting their perception of the person as truth, misunderstanding will often result. Sometimes I'll ask students if they ever saw or met someone for the first time and thought "I don't think I like this kid" and later that same person became one of their closest friends. Many will agree this has happened.

I have used Jim Lew's "Feature Films" process and other perspective challenges with students to emphasize the point of how important it is to seek out ways to really understand the differences that exist among people by imagining what others might be thinking and feeling. Imagination is a step to understanding—a step to making a connection which becomes more lasting when someone enters into conversation with another to either affirm or discount one's perceptions. An excellent resource for teaching perspective is a book by Nancy Schniedewind and Ellen Davidson, *Cooperative Learning, Cooperative Lives* (see the Additional Resources on page 213).

What Is Empathy?

When I was 7 years old, my father took me to a baseball game at Shea Stadium in New York City. The memory that stands out for me from that day has nothing to do with the game. Instead, I remember an incident that took place in the seats in front of us. An older man was sitting in someone else's seat. He probably misread his ticket and was in the wrong aisle or section. When the person who was supposed to sit there found his seat occupied, he started screaming at the man. I remember watching the face of the man who had sat in the wrong seat. He seemed flustered, confused, and embarrassed. I remember thinking, Why is that man being so mean? For the rest of the game, I couldn't get the older man out of my mind. I found myself wondering how he was and where he was sitting and whether he was okay. I kept looking for him to see where he was sitting. I wanted him to be okay. I wanted him to have a good time. I can still see the face of that man in my mind. I remember the straw golf cap he wore with the NY insignia in orange, his pained facial expression. That experience and its accompanying emotional memory has symbolized for me what happens when an empathic urge to do something is not acted upon: we might move on from the experience, but we will never forget it.

Empathy has become such a common term in so much of the literature about preventing and reducing aggression and violence in schools that what empathy really means can become a bit clouded at times. Empathy begins as an emotional or visceral response to another person's anxious or painful event, and then moves to feeling as if that event is one's own—that it is actually happening to oneself. The feeling of empathy evolves into a skill when the empathizer wants to help the other person with compassionate words or responsive acts, such as listening intently. It is quite natural to have an emotional response when someone else is in distress or feeling confused or frustrated. The empathy process in its simplest form takes place when a person's emotional response translates into a caring action.

Some key phrases in the definition of empathy are in *The Prepare Curriculum: Teaching Prosocial Competencies* (Goldstein, 1999):

Feeling into _____

Appreciation for_____

- Role taking

- Perspective taking

- Imaginatively putting yourself into another person's place

- Perceptual, reverberatory, and cognitive analysis

- Communicating with another _____.
  (pp. 629–642)

Goldstein quotes Cotu as saying that "empathy is the process by which a person momentarily pretends to himself that he is another person, projects himself into the perceptual field of the other person, [and] imaginatively puts himself in the other person's place" (p. 629). Cotu's use of the verb "projecting" conjures up the image of watching a movie of someone else's life using an old-fashioned *projector* and movie screen. The viewer becomes completely absorbed into the movie and is able to think, feel, and sense as though he or she were the person projected on the film. Indeed, one effective technique for teaching empathy is through role reversal during a role play. For instance, one social situation that often occurs is the arrival of a new student after the school year has begun. The many kinds of events that may have precipitated the new student's move—such things as a family breakup, loss of a job by one of the parents, or a forced transfer by a parent's employer—exacerbate this stressful situation. Before the new student arrives, the teacher can express his or her concern to the class in a general way, saying something like, "It must be difficult to come to a new school—especially after the year has already started. Let's role-play what a new student might be thinking and feeling." Doing this will help students gain a greater sense of understanding for the incoming student and will empower them to do something supportive for the newcomer, thereby activating an empathic, generous, and community-centered response.

The Importance of Ritual

In the truest sense of community spirit, a process for welcoming newcomers can be ingrained into the culture as a ritual that is designed and carried out by the students. A ritual of this sort helps create a way of thinking as a form of perspective taking. Acknowledging and celebrating a student's birthday is another example of ritual: a ceremony shared with the entire community. Feelings of connection and safety are strengthened any time a person is recognized, acknowledged, and appreciated.

Empathy as a Heart Skill

I have had many conversations with teachers and other education and youth professionals about whether empathy is a skill and, if so, how it can be taught most effectively. Some feel that it is an innate gift that is more touch than skill. In their book *Executive EQ: Emotional Intelligence in Leadership and Organizations* (1997), Robert Cooper and Ayman Sawaf offer compassion as empathy's companion, stating:

> *Through feelings of empathy and compassion we help ourselves learn and grow, and we also enable others to begin to feel safe enough to talk about what is really going on in their lives—to tell their stories—without fear of being judged, criticized or abandoned. It is then that we begin to empathize with them, and extend compassion and support to them. (p. 48)*

The acts that make up the essence of empathy are presence, focus, hearing, and reflection. Empathy is most often associated with a feeling, but it is actually a skill made up of a series of strategies. The key is for these strategies to be motivated from within rather than to be driven from without, such as someone *telling* a student, "How would you feel if someone did that to you?" Empathy in its purest form is natural and from the heart; it is a heart skill. When a toddler hears another child crying, for example, the toddler will immediately notice and ask, "Why is she crying?" The toddler may even take the crying child to his or her mother for attention. These natural, heartfelt human responses come from concern and compassion.

During the course of a child's life, this natural empathic state becomes overridden as the child learns other social survival strategies such as who to be friends with in order to gain acceptance, what clothes to wear, what to say, or simply how to avoid those kids who are hassled by others even if he or she feels compassion and concern for them. Therefore, teaching empathy is often a process of reverberation in which the learner is returned to a memory of the feeling he or she once felt so naturally.

The Value of Storytelling

There is a theory that everyone on earth is separated by no more than six degrees of separation. This idea can be applied to personal stories. When someone tells a story of something that happened to them, many in the room will have experienced something very similar. Although it is not their immediate story, it could be. In that way, they are not that far removed from the feelings involved and from the actions that need to be taken. This dynamic is enhanced when the teacher shares a personal story during a social decision making lesson. This sharing heightens the students' perception of their teacher as human while opening the students up to the meaning of the lesson learned from the teacher's experience.

An empathic dialogue or social discovery lesson can take place when a teacher tells a story that takes students back in time to an event that is familiar for many—such as not being invited to a birthday party. Even if students have never directly experienced the disappointment of such an isolating event (or if students are unwilling to admit it), this seemingly trivial past experience can shed a bright light on the need that all people have to be included and to fit in. The pain, frustration, and confusion often associated with being left out has been felt by each of us. These strong feelings lead to the question many of us have had to answer at some time in our lives in relation to another person's situation: What is the right thing to do?

The most significant learning stories are found within a teacher's own treasure trove of personal life experiences. After all, the oral tradition of storytelling is the oldest form of teaching by an elder to an initiate (a young person moving toward the passage into adulthood), providing the elder with the opportunity to teach about life from a position of wisdom and experience. In our classrooms, the elder is the teacher (even in the first year) and the initiate is the student. If the story is to prove effective, it must be relevant and authentic—one that models self-reflection and personal growth for the storyteller.

I often share how I was teased by my friends in fifth grade for being short and how this continued all the way through high school with the same group of kids. These childhood experiences through the years have had a huge impact on me. One reflection I often share is that I learned the importance in being careful about who I call a friend. Someone who hurts my feelings and teases me when I do not want them to is not someone I would consider a friend. What I do look for in my friends is someone who demonstrates caring by listening, encouraging, and supporting without judging. Whatever the story and accompanying lesson, when teachers integrate personal storytelling into the lesson, students will often experience heart-felt empathic responses.

Beware of Blind Spots

Storytelling can create opportunities for increased understanding of oneself and others by successfully turning on the

"Aha! light" to clarify another person's perception of events. The "Aha! light" is a metaphor for the moment of discovery that is sparked when a person sees things in another way for the first time. This illumination provides alternative viewpoints and a clearer sense of truth—what is actually happening—for a young person who is in the middle of making a difficult social decision.

In his seminal work, *The 7 Habits of Highly Effective People: Powerful Lessons in Personal Change*, Stephen Covey (1989) tells of an experience he had one Sunday morning while riding a subway in New York. When this story is effectively told to a group of students, it touches their hearts and opens their minds to the notion that everyone has a story to tell. Rather than judge, label, or act intolerantly toward someone whose behavior they do not understand, students realize they can choose to respond with compassion, generosity, and empathy in an effort to learn more. Covey writes:

> *People were sitting quietly—some reading newspapers, some lost in thought, some resting with their eyes closed. It was a calm, peaceful scene.*
>
> *Then suddenly, a man and his children entered the subway car. The children were so loud and rambunctious that instantly the whole climate changed.*
>
> *The man sat down next to me and closed his eyes, apparently oblivious to the situation. The children were yelling back and forth, throwing things, even grabbing people's papers. It was very disturbing. And yet, the man sitting next to me did nothing.*

At this point, I stop the story to ask for student input and reflection on several questions:

- What must Stephen Covey and the other passengers have thought and felt about the father who let his kids run wild on the subway?

- What labels, judgments, or intolerant thoughts might the passengers have had?

- What are your impressions of the kids?

After a brief dialogue spurred on by my questions, I continue with Covey's story:

> *It was difficult not to feel irritated. I could not believe that he could be so insensitive as to let his children run wild like that and do nothing about it, taking no responsibility at all. It was easy to see that everyone else on the subway felt irritated, too. So finally, with what I felt was unusual patience and restraint, I turned to him and said, "Sir, your children are really disturbing a lot of people. I wonder if you couldn't control them a little more?"*

> *The man lifted his gaze as if to come to a consciousness of the situation for the first time and said softly, "Oh, you're right. I guess I should do something about it. We just came from the hospital where their mother died about an hour ago. I don't know what to think, and I guess they don't know how to handle it either."*

> . . . *"Your wife just died? Oh, I'm so sorry! Can you*
> *tell me about it? What can I do to help?"* Everything
> *changed in an instant.* (pp. 30–31)

"Everything changed in an instant"—it often does when one takes the time to get all of the information in any given situation. Suddenly, a person's perception changes and the "light bulb" of understanding comes on and he or she may say, "Oh, I get it." That moment of getting it is the "Aha! light" turning on.

The Gifts of Compassion, Wisdom, and Modeling

It is possible to respond with empathy before you understand the entire story. In the story of the man and his children on the train, Stephen Covey responded with greater empathy when he learned about the man's situation. The ability to respond with empathy before you understand comes down to intention and focused concentration on events and people. If you are with a person or a group of people and something does not seem right, it probably is not right. Often when I'm facilitating a group of adults, if someone does not seem to be in synch with the group or seems disinterested and upset, I will look at the person and gently ask if everything is okay or if they have something to say. People appreciate this because my actions communicate that I am noticing that person and am not judging him or her. The person may still be upset but he or she has permission to feel that way.

I remember being a seventh grader in an advanced algebra class and feeling overwhelmed by the material. One classmate named Tom helped me study for our midterm exam. After the test, I thought I had done well. I understood the material and could hardly wait until the next class when tests would be returned. Unfortunately, I had mixed up a few formulas and failed the exam. When I saw the failing grade at the top of the page, I put my head down on my desk and wished I could disappear. I felt so embarrassed and disappointed in myself. Suddenly, I noticed someone standing beside me and I heard Tom ask, "What went wrong, Dave?" I looked up almost in tears and saw him looking at me with caring and compassion. He looked as if *he* had just failed the test. "You're going to be okay," he continued. "You know this stuff. You just have to keep working on it. I'll help you."

I'll never forget Tom's genuine, heartfelt response. It gave me strength that day in a vulnerable moment, and it is an emotional memory that has stayed with me all of these years.

Recently, while I taught a social skills lesson to fifth graders, a girl named Stella spontaneously began to cry as she shared with the class that she was often teased in school. The group became silent and reflective. I also waited silently and then asked if anyone had anything to say to Stella. Two girls offered her words of support and one boy, Jonah, spoke up and said, "I know that Stella isn't such a great athlete, but she is a great violinist." Jonah continued, "Everyone in this circle has a gift, and my mom says that's what we have to think about—our strengths, not our weaknesses." Jonah's sharing reflected the valuable wisdom his mother had shared with him and also indicated that his mother's words had reverberated deeply within his understanding of himself and others.

Heartfelt reverberation must also be exhibited and expressed by the teacher toward his or her students. In this sense, to reverberate means to reflect back. For the teacher, this means that he or she is "person-centered." The teacher is present and available for students, especially during times of trauma and stress. The teacher should listen carefully to the troubled student, act non-judgmentally, reflect a sense of compassion that indicates he or she understands what the student is going through, and help the student devise a plan for what should be done next. The teacher who displays heartfelt reverberation is someone who is empathic and able to establish trust with students. This starts with the ability to listen intently and allow students to talk without interruption. Val Mihic, special education teacher and educational consultant, shared with me the following story, which shows this kind of reverberation in action:

> *One year, after returning from our holiday vacation, Michael, one of my students, was telling others in the class about the Nintendo® game he had received for Christmas. It soon became apparent that Michael was not telling the others the truth; that he really had not received a Nintendo®. The other kids knew this as well and started to make fun of him. I sensed Michael's pain and I knew he had a story to tell. I spoke with Michael privately asking him if he had in fact received a Nintendo® for a gift. He said "no" and then told me how he hadn't received much for Christmas; how his parents had an argument on Christmas Eve and his stepfather left the house that night. Michael said he didn't want the others to make fun of him so he made up the story of the Nintendo®.*

In this story, Michael was too embarrassed and hurt to tell the truth about his meager and disappointing Christmas. He *made up a story* when in truth he needed the opportunity to *tell his story*. His teacher asked if he would like to talk to the class about the situation. Michael agreed. During a class meeting where the class was seated in a focused circle, he told his true story. When Michael explained that his holiday had been a major disappointment for him, he was embraced emotionally by classmates who said such things to him as "Don't worry about not getting anything, Michael. You can use my Nintendo®." This moment of "group empathy" was initiated through the empathic actions of Michael's teacher, Val Mihic.

Empathy is an intuitive process that can be cultivated. It requires a person to be present when spending time with another and to listen. Being present in this context means coming into the relationship with the intention of caring: wanting to help the other person through listening, support, and encouragement. The fact that Val was "present" with his student is what caused him to speak to Michael in the way that he did. When a teacher is present for his or her students, this presence carries with it the opportunity for appreciation, thereby opening the door for an *empathic moment* to be shared between two individuals—a moment that can be filled with the extremes of joy and elation, sorrow and disappointment. The result of this empathic moment is summed up eloquently in the Swedish proverb (www.thinkexist.com):

> *Shared joy is a double joy;*
> *Shared sorrow is half a sorrow.*

One empathic moment can significantly alter the course of a person's life, propelling him or her toward a new destination with a renewed sense of optimism and hope.

In *Kids Who Outwit Adults,* Larry Brendtro and John Seita (2004) observed that "often we plant therapeutic seeds that may bear belated fruit. We know that the brain constructs our life stories by selecting and remembering crucial events that have major influences on the path of our lives" (p. 151). When an incident has occurred with a student, there is always a story behind it—a sequence of events that led to the incident. When students are encouraged to do so by the teacher, the sharing of one's individual story helps create a sacred or honorable climate in which teaching, learning, and community building occur. It is the teacher's responsibility to intentionally create a setting in which storytelling—the sharing and *understanding* of other people's realities—is nurtured.

In the book *The Sacred: Ways of Knowledge, Sources of Life* (1977), Peggy V. Beck, A. L. Walters, and Nia Francisco write about the Lakota Sioux oral tradition of storytelling and how the Lakota consider storytelling to be the most significant practice for teaching the ways of the world and the ways of their people (pp. 58-63). I have found that learning about the traditions of the Native Americans has intrigued, opened up, and inspired many young people in my classes. Students find great fascination with the organic nature of happiness and purpose, which is embraced through the creation of, and devotion to, caring relationships toward one's self, others in the group or tribe, and the environment. I often use Native American stories as symbols for teaching the honorable intentions of empathy, compassion, appreciation, generosity, and even soul expression. Soul expression is when someone feels a strong passion about what they want to do in life and is able to pursue meaningful goals toward that end, such as being inspired to craft a beautiful piece of furniture, play a musical instrument, play a sport, fix cars, write a poem, or work in a scientific field to create something that will make a difference in the world. In the Lakota tradition, most of the significant teaching and storytelling took place around the fire.

> *The whole situation, the atmosphere around the fire, was dramatic—different from ordinary things like daily conversation and instruction. Maria Chona, a Papago woman, explains how a child learned among her people: "My father went on talking to me in a low voice. This is how our people always talk to their children, so low and quiet, the child thinks he is dreaming. But he never forgets."* (Beck, Walters, & Francisco, 1977, p. 60)

For more valuable information concerning Native American stories and traditions, refer to *The Lakota Way: Stories and Lessons for Living* (2001) by Joseph M. Marshall, III, and *The Legend of the Indian Paintbrush* (1988), retold by Tomie dePaola (see Additional Resources on page 213).

I am certain that Val's student Michael never forgot what his teacher did for him so many years ago. Val, the teacher, taught Michael, the student, that there is a place for each person and a place for each story. Michael's classmates learned this as well. Inviting Michael to share his story in a class meeting is analogous to the "dramatic and different" (and empathic) atmosphere described by Maria Chona in the passage above. Speaking in a low dreamlike voice symbolically means to intentionally create a nonjudgmental, emotionally safe teacher-student relationship that facilitates a learning environment where everyone feels an attachment to the group. It feels dreamlike because the feelings of safety, connection, and belonging are everyone's dream or desire.

Symbolic Teaching and
Real-Time Learning

When filtered through the lens of a student, a lesson on the social dynamics of belonging, fitting in, and making healthy choices could quickly turn into a lecture on right and wrong, ultimately turning students off to the potential for meaningful dialogue. And yet anyone who has been around young people on a regular basis marvels at the way they often are able to make lucid connections to a variety of scenarios, putting things into a framework that makes sense.

Social Learning theorist Albert Bandura, in his book *Self-Efficacy: The Exercise of Control* (1997), notes that "a great deal of information about human values, thinking patterns, and behavior . . . is gained from models portrayed symbolically" (p. 440). The application of specific rules of social behavior is not an easy task. Not all social situations are *fixed* or constant when put into practice but rather are *generative* or improvised based on a number of variables. If, during the course of a social skills lesson, the rule of behavior is presented symbolically, as Bandura points out, then there is room for truth in application—meaning there is a greater chance to create a realistic and lasting impression for the learner (Bandura, 1997, p. 440).

Symbolic learning strengthens one's symbolic vision. Symbolic vision means to step back from the immediacy of events to see a bigger picture, a life lesson. The ideal scenario is for the student to generalize and apply the social skill lesson in a variety of real school-life situations throughout the day by tapping into his or her newfound awareness or alternative way of thinking and acting. One effective, symbolic social skills teaching method is to hold a moral dilemma discussion in which a situation with numerous ethical or moral angles is presented. The group dialogues about the situation and individuals make their own decisions. This is consistent with the understanding that "appropriate sub-skills are flexibly orchestrated to fit the demands of particular situations" (Bandura, 1997, p. 440). These sub-skills might also be called emotional competencies. These are covered in section 2.

Moral dilemma discussions often engage the learner in exploring new areas of consideration. If the experience creates feelings that are strong enough, the experience may be wired directly to that child's perception of the world in the form of an emotional memory, thus affecting the child's future choices and behaviors. Some people, such as my classmate Tom from seventh grade, have a natural inclination toward caring and empathic behaviors. Others will benefit from group conversations in which various social options are identified, explored, and practiced.

The Lost Wallet

Although it can be humbling at times, a teacher who shares the primary experience of personal storytelling with his or her students offers them a unique perspective on the daily experiences the teacher has had with others.

Discovery through story and reflective dialogue provides for an authentic, co-creative learning experience. It also strengthens the feeling of community while modeling healthy and caring options instead of aggressive and negatively charged ones.

I often teach by sharing experiences that I or others close to me have had. Here is an example of a recent experience my family went through:

My wife, Jodi, left her wallet on the roof of her car as she was putting our son, Sam, into his baby seat. Jodi had just returned from the bank and had $800 in her wallet so that she could wire the money to pay a bill via Western Union®. When she arrived at the Western Union office without her wallet, she quickly returned to the bank parking lot to search for it.

Jodi called me later in the day. Of course, I was upset to learn about the loss of such a large sum of money. My 90-minute drive home gave me time for reflection, and I soon became more concerned about my wife's feelings than the loss of money. In other words, I moved into an empathic mode.

After my arrival home, I was comforting my wife when we received a phone call from someone who said he had found Jodi's wallet earlier in the day. We drove to the man's house to retrieve the wallet and found the entire $800 intact.

The man who found Jodi's wallet was working at a construction site. He found her wallet in the road as he was driving to a deli on his lunch break. He said he did not have access to a phone at his work site and was, therefore, unable to call until later in the day.

I asked him why he had returned the wallet with all of the money and he said, "I know how it must have felt to lose that wallet with so much money, and I hope if something like this ever happens to me, someone will return my wallet."

The next day I told my sixth-grade class my wife's story. Not only were the students completely focused on the real-life events which had happened the previous day, but they were also fascinated with the choice made by the person who returned the wallet. Together we "unpacked" or relived the story, starting with how my wife felt about the loss of the money and moving on to how I initially reacted when I learned about the events—first being upset with the loss and then being concerned about my wife's feelings. We discussed what I did when I saw my wife, and we considered the entire scenario through the eyes of the man who found the wallet. The most spirited dialogue took place when I asked the following questions:

1. What would you have done if you had found the wallet?

2. What if the man who found the wallet had kept the money but anonymously mailed the wallet back along with credit cards, driver's license, and so on? How would the man have felt? Would this have been acceptable behavior?

3. How do you think the man felt after he returned the wallet?

4. What would you have said to him?

5. Have you ever been in a similar situation, either losing money or finding it and returning it?

The conversation which we shared became a lesson rich in empathy, morals, and decision making as well as in the challenge of embracing hope and optimism in the middle of a stressful event.

I told this story to my students with my wife's good wishes. We both felt that its happy ending teaches that goodness does exist in the world.

A Caring Presence

Whenever I tell the story of the lost wallet, all sides of the "finder's" response are explored: returning the money, returning just the credit cards and driver's license, or keeping the money and throwing the wallet away. One time when I shared the story with one group of students, a boy said that my wife was careless and that she deserved to lose the money and was even a bad mother. My initial urge was to defend my wife and reprimand the boy. If I had scolded the student, however, I would have lost any chance to facilitate a successful lesson with him *and* the rest of the group.

At this point in the lesson, we were in the middle of a moral dilemma dialogue in which I had said there were no easy answers. My challenge was to support the student for having an opinion, disconnect emotionally from what he was saying, and model acceptance by exploring why he felt the way he did. As it turned out, I didn't have to defend my wife. Most of the students did that for me. Although I had the inner turmoil of being bothered by the student's remarks, my position of being the accepting, nonjudgmental teacher remained intact.

The key to emotionally safe schools lies in the intentional positive cultivation of the multitude of relationships that make up the school experience. The critical players are the teachers, administrators, and other staff members. Whatever social behaviors are modeled by the adults in the school will not only be observed and experienced by the students but will also be learned by them. Sarcasm, for example, has no place in school, no matter whether it is used as a humorous strategy or as a controlling tactic. Sarcasm intimidates and bullies the students, and the staff member who relies on this approach does an injustice to his or her students by teaching sarcasm as a social strategy.

Empathy, on the other hand, must be modeled and practiced as an integral part of teaching with the intention of transferring empathy into a student's way of thinking and acting. Positive youth development is about strength-based interventions: meeting kids where they are and building on their existing strengths. An initial step in a strength-based intervention is to identify something the child enjoys, such as a talent, a gift, or a special interest. Once this has been determined, the child can be provided with multiple opportunities to experience this gift. This approach appeals to the child's view of the world and his or her place in that world; it appeals to his or her "private logic." I recently met a bilingual teacher, Rebecca, who told me the following story that illustrates this idea:

> I grew up in a small village in Mexico. When I was around 9 years old, I quit my gymnastics class because I wasn't very good at making the moves—it wasn't fun for me. The teacher of the class moved back to Mexico City and soon the new teacher visited me. Although I wasn't good at the gymnastic moves, I was very good at sequencing. I could remember all of the steps in the proper order for each of the routines. The new teacher came to ask me if I could help her teach the steps to the other students in the class. I agreed, and thereafter had a positive experience. To this day, I continue to

*have significant memories about gymnastics—memories
brought on by someone who responded to my strengths
rather than my weaknesses.*

Strength-based interventions are strategies that reflect a high
degree of empathy. Someone who uses a strength-based intervention is able to see *through the eyes* of the student and in the
process build a protective relationship that is safe and encouraging—one that provides a sense of optimism and hope for the
future.

Empathy as Imagination

The best way for a teacher to connect, motivate, and inspire
a student toward social discovery is to take enough of an interest in that student so that the teacher knows what the student is
going through and can imagine what he or she is experiencing
and feeling on a much deeper level. Most teachers want to establish rapport with their students. Most teachers attempt this by
taking a personal interest in their kids, by knowing what is going
on not only in their classroom but in all of their students' other
classes as well.

It is not necessary to have experienced an identical situation
as another person or even to completely understand it in order
to relate to what is going on with that person. If a person has had
a similar situation, that is all that is necessary. Imagination is a
form of empathy that allows someone to feel and experience the
emotions of another, serving as a rung on the ladder toward
empathic action. In fact, one of the most empathic questions to
ask a group of students is, "Can you imagine what that person(s)
must have been feeling?" This is asked not as an accusation but
rather as a discovery tool for understanding. At workshops for

teachers, I have often used the following story about a boy named Tom from James Garbarino and Ellen deLara's book, *And Words Can Hurt Forever: How to Protect Adolescents from Bullying, Harassment, and Emotional Violence* (2002):

> *When Tom was in seventh grade, he walked into his English class and overheard his teacher and a colleague discussing his paper, laughing and commenting negatively. At first they didn't see him, so he heard more than he should have, and certainly more than they had intended. Tom was crushed. He had no idea that teachers would ever laugh about a student, or that his work would be the subject of a joke.*
>
> *After that he gave up trying and became a mediocre student, even though in elementary school he had received straight A's. Years later, he remembers this event vividly and with pain as the turning point in his academic career.* (p. 26)

Can you imagine how Tom must have felt? If you had Tom as a student and heard that this had happened with one of the teachers on your team or in your school, what would you say? What would you do? Chances are, after considering what happened to him, your feelings and any actions you would consider would be driven by feelings of empathy and compassion for Tom.

Empathy is an "outside-in" dynamic that begins with the *outside experience* of another and, when focused upon, enters *into the heart* of the empathizer. In Tom's situation, it is hard not to feel the utter discouragement, disappointment, and disillusionment he must have felt. His story creates a sensory experience of pain and perhaps outrage that tugs at one's heart. When a teacher says something like "My heart goes out to that kid" or finds him- or herself unconsciously putting a hand over the heart, the deeply symbolic words and actions are expressing the sensory experience of a teacher's empathic imagination.

From Alienation to Connection: Shaping a Student's Life

It is an extremely painful experience for students to feel disconnected from a group of other students or their teachers or from a place like a school or classroom. Those experiencing this kind of pain will often talk about it and will express their desire for the pain to go away. As depth psychologist and VisionQuest® guide Bill Plotkin has said in a training experience I had, "When the soul wants to change, it shows up in scary shapes." In the world of a school, these "scary shapes" can manifest themselves as either antisocial behaviors or a seeming lack of desire to achieve.

A friend of mine attended a parent conference for his son, Greg, who was then in the sixth grade. In reference to Greg not completing his homework, his teacher said, "It's obvious that Gregory doesn't care about doing his homework." What the teacher did not understand was that Greg cared deeply about his work but was frustrated because he had to work considerably longer than his twin brother each night in an effort to accomplish his homework. Even with all of the extra time he spent, Greg received lower grades than his brother. The problem was not that Greg did not care, but that he felt frustrated that he did not "measure up." Two years later, Greg had an eighth-grade teacher who helped him discover a special interest and ability in social studies. This newfound achievement turned Greg around, and he began to feel confidence in himself and "care" about his work. That one experience of "connection" was the spark needed to turn things around for Greg. Incidentally, the teacher who helped Greg discover his way in the eighth grade was the person who had attended the parent conference 2 years earlier—his father.

Irish philosopher and poet John O'Donohue compares a person's life potential to a piece of clay that can be molded into any shape imaginable. Speaking figuratively, teachers who establish empathic relationships with their students will sense what types of "clay" each child represents and reflect this information back to the students, thereby helping each young person mold his or her unique shape, life expression, and future direction. Of life expression and self-trust, O'Donohue (2005) writes:

> There is an unseen life that dreams us: it knows our true destiny. We can trust ourselves more than we realize and we need have no fear of change. We can risk everything for growth and we'll never be disappointed.

Full Humanness

American psychologist Abraham Maslow (1971) became fascinated with human developmental needs and with reaching one's potential when he found himself admiring two of his teachers whom he "could not be content to simply adore but sought to understand." This quest to comprehend the special qualities of these teachers started Maslow's research to determine the essence of the place of "full humanness" (pp. 40-41) that he felt his two teachers held.

Maslow is most well-known for his theory of the Hierarchy of Needs. He perceived that humans are motivated by unsatisfied needs and that lower needs must be satisfied before higher needs can be fulfilled. The highest level on the hierarchy is to be self-actualized. Of self-actualization and full humanness, he writes that "self-actualization means experiencing fully, vividly, selflessly, with full concentration and total absorption. . . . At this moment of experiencing, the person is wholly and fully human." (p. 44)

Achieving "full humanness" is a worthy objective for teachers. From this position they can do for their students what Maslow's teachers did for him: inspire them to a place of integrity, joy, creativity, and caring expression. These are the qualities that make up the empathic experience.

The Circle of Courage

In the book *Reclaiming Youth At Risk: Our Hope for the Future*, Larry Brendtro, Martin Brokenleg, and Steve Van Bockern (2002) present their youth developmental framework called the Circle of Courage™. Dr. Brokenleg wrote the following about its inception: "In 1988 we were asked by the Child Welfare League of America to make a presentation on Native American child development principles to an international conference in Washington, DC. We called our synthesis of this research on tribal wisdom the Circle of Courage" (1998, p. 131). Within the Circle are four developmental needs: belonging, mastery, independence, and generosity. The authors of *Reclaiming Youth at Risk* use the term "reclaim" to identify the challenge we face when working with a young person who is *discouraged* or outside of the Circle. As significant adults in a discouraged child's life, teachers can reclaim a student to his or her rightful place of full humanness by finding ways to meet the student's emotional needs, thereby welcoming him or her back into the Circle of Courage.

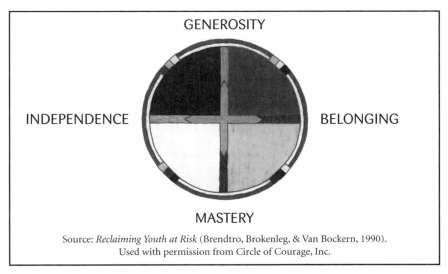

GENEROSITY

INDEPENDENCE   BELONGING

MASTERY

Source: *Reclaiming Youth at Risk* (Brendtro, Brokenleg, & Van Bockern, 1990).
Used with permission from Circle of Courage, Inc.

The Circle of Courage provides a clear view into the world of choices and shows why empathic choices make sense on the cognitive level but not necessarily on the emotional level. I have taught the Circle by referring to the basketball game known as "Around the World." In this game each person starts out in the same place—the need for belonging. Once belonging is achieved, the person moves to the next spot on the Circle, which is the place of mastery or learning new skills (in this case, the skills of empathy and compassion). In the basketball game, if a person misses a shot, he may "take a chance," meaning if he shoots again and makes the shot, he moves on, but if he misses he must return to the starting point. This is analogous to reaching out to someone who has few friends. In doing this a person is taking the chance of losing his or her friends and going back to the beginning— feeling the need for belonging, just like in the basketball game. The fear of losing one's friends and being rejected by others is the main reason most students often "look the other way" when they notice another person being rejected or ridiculed.

The true test of strength or courage is to move on to the next phase in the Circle of Courage—independence, which essentially means putting into practice the skills and beliefs (principles) a person has achieved. It is one thing to be able to give the right answers in class during a conversation concerning empathy and reaching out to others, but it is quite another to demonstrate these "right answers" in real life in what Arnold Goldstein has called "the anxiety of the moment" (Goldstein, 1996, personal comment/workshop). Once a student is able to act from the place of independence, the final and most rewarding place in the Circle is achieved—generosity.

Generosity means to truly act out with unselfish, altruistic acts. That is exactly what empathy is. In the Circle of Courage, generosity is the gateway back to a solid place of belonging. It provides a highly positive meaning to the phrase "what goes around comes around." I often share my belief with students that, many times, the people who others are attracted to—the ones they like and seek out—are those who are kind and considerate because these are the people others enjoy being with, and they feel safe with them. Some people, however, are stuck in one direction of the wheel, usually in the place of mastery. They understand the ideas and reasons behind empathic acts cognitively but they are unable to risk making emotionally challenging social choices, fearing the loss of status or place within their peer group. They do not want to lose their friends.

Whenever someone is stuck on one point or direction within the Circle, the strategy for becoming unstuck is to travel in the opposite direction and work within that developmental need. The Native Americans call this type of work a Medicine Task. In fact, the Circle of Courage is a version of what the Native Americans call the medicine wheel (www.crystalinks.com/bighorn.html). It is felt that emotional healing or "wholeness" takes place within the wheel. In the Circle of Courage, for example, when someone is stuck in the south (mastery), the teacher can provide that person with a northern (generous) experience such as using a skill one has to help others. A student who is masterful at building models of cars can build a model with a younger student. This is an act of mastery (the ability to build a model) within the context of generosity (sharing with a younger student).

The previous example provides the rationale for creating a student mentoring program in which older students mentor younger ones. When an older class teams up with a younger one for shared experiences throughout the year, this mentoring represents a group of masters generously sharing their gifts.

The ideas of caring and being nice to others are not new concepts for students. Although these concepts have been discussed in many ways for many years, we still need to stress that choices toward others (including the words people use) do have consequences, often long-term ones. The emotional stress caused by the *antisocial behaviors* of teasing, harassment, and bullying reflects a form of emotional violence (Garbarino & deLara, 2002, pp. 23–24). Teachers must never stop looking for the most effective ways to teach the *pro-social skills* of empathy, compassion, caring, and generosity.

For Real

There's a hole in the middle of the prettiest life,
So the lawyers and the prophets say,
Not your father, nor your mother,
Nor your lover's gonna ever make it go away,
And there's too much darkness in an endless night
To be afraid of the way we feel,
Let's be kind to each other, not forever, but for real.

—Bob Franke © 1983 Telephone Pole Music (BMI)
(used by permission)

Sometimes there is a hole in a student's life which comes from the yearning for meaning from what is going on in school. Often school programs such as character education and bully prevention begin with the best of intentions but prove to be counterproductive because they trivialize what they are supposed to be affecting. Being "for real" means more than a program or curriculum. It means the creation of a tender way of being, a culture which acts to soften the edges around the harshness of what life often delivers. This way of being authentically seeks to create a caring and compassionate elder-initiate relationship that uses the teaching methods of trust, modeling, support, and intentional emotional imprinting.

In *The Tipping Point* (2000), Malcolm Gladwell writes of the broken windows theory of crime identified by criminologists James Q. Wilson and George Kelling:

> *Wilson and Kelling argued that crime is the inevitable result of disorder. If a window is broken or left unrepaired, people walking by will conclude that no one cares and no one is in charge. Soon more windows will*

be broken, and the sense of anarchy will spread from the building to the street on which it faces, sending a signal that anything goes. (p. 141)

The "broken windows" in the world of a school are the broken relationships that need to be repaired—one at a time. These are the students who are unconnected, labeled, and judged—students like Bob—that are written off as difficult and unmotivated. These students need and deserve the chance to tell their untold stories and to demonstrate who they truly are. When the importance of human relationships is minimized, then as the broken windows theory suggests, intolerance, an unsafe environment, and blame will be the cultural norm, no matter how many award-winning programs exist or how many school safety training days have been completed.

In the next section, section 2, the focus moves toward exercises and processes for effectively teaching empathy and its companion skills to students. This section considers how we must remain hopeful, courageous, and grounded in our work with students by using specific, focused, and relevant social skills teaching methods and approaches.

Section 2

Learning Empathy: Facilitating Social Discovery

You want to be friendly,
funny, and smart.
You try to fit in,
but where do you start?
Your friends are all laughing,
sharing some news.
You join in the laughter.
You haven't a clue.
Who am I?
I really should know.
I have so many faces.
Which one should I show?

—From a Song Written by Three Seventh-Grade
Students in Attleboro, Massachusetts

Introduction to Social Skills Learning

A principal at a middle school recently told me he felt that the middle school curriculum should concern itself only with social issues. "They're going to get the academics all over again in high school," he said. "At this age, all they're concerned with is what's going on with their peers."

Of course, he and I both knew this could never happen in the age of standards and high-stakes testing, and yet I took his point to mean that *within* this time of assessments and standards, we must not discount the social and emotional development of our students and the sense of hope and purpose which the school experience can provide. Thomas J. Sergiovanni (2004) wrote in the article "Building a Community of Hope" about the importance of hope:

> *Too often hope is overlooked or misunderstood. Modern management theory tells us that the only results that count are those you can see and compute—not those you can feel. According to this theory, we must be objective: look at hard evidence before we dare to believe, think, or judge; and in other ways blindly face reality. "If it can't be measured," the saying goes, "it can't be managed."*
>
> *Why tie our hands and discourage our hearts when we know that hope can make a difference? Educators can be both hopeful and realistic as long as the possibilities for change remain open. Being realistic differs from facing reality in important ways. Facing reality means accepting the inevitability of a situation or circumstance; being realistic means*

calculating the odds with an eye toward optimism.
(pp. 33–34)

We may not always see the fruits of our hopeful thinking regarding a student's social choices, but a first, optimistic step is to realize that we can note levels of cognitive awareness that could lead to different choices in the future: ones we had a hand in shaping.

Teaching pro-social skills is not an "add-on" to the curriculum. Instead, it is a realistic and critical component of the school experience that helps students become "realistic" regarding the multitude of life's changes. Section 1 focused on the school and the adults in the school as key players in establishing a caring, empathic culture. This section presents a process I have used to effectively teach social skills through the facilitation of what I call *social discovery lessons*. A successful social skills lesson is more appropriately called a discovery lesson because an effective experience will guide students toward their own discoveries about their peer relationships and their place in the world. Social discovery takes place through a meaningful and optimistic conversation between the teacher and class. This section also includes specific information on emotional intelligence (EI). When one's EI competencies are strengthened, a higher degree of empathy is strengthened as well.

Courageous Conversations

Poet David Whyte speaks of the need to carry forth a courageous conversation in which an individual periodically checks in with him- or herself, asking the hard questions about one's life and the choices one has within that life in order to reach the frontier of one's own experience (Whyte, 2001, p. 14). In the classroom, a courageous conversation is facilitated when the teacher is able to articulate the truths inherent in the life experience, essentially focusing on the need all people have to be connected to others, to be cool and to have friends, and to recognize how this social need is a constant presence within our thoughts each day. This seemingly obvious observation can be absolutely profound for the "persons in process"—a name we give to our students in these courageous conversations.

If our classroom conversations are courageous or "heartfelt"—which is how David Whyte describes courage, derived from the "old French *cuer,* meaning heart" (p. 14)—then the opportunity for deep meaning and lifelong application will have been unearthed. Recently, after a lesson I called "Courageous Conversations" with a class of fifth-grade students, a girl came up to me and said, "This is like a subject. What we talk about is like doing science or social studies. I wish we had this as a subject every day in school." Her point is well taken. Like many of her classmates, she wants to know about life on her terms, with her stories or reflections mirrored back in caring and thoughtful ways.

What a concept—offering a subject in school called Courageous Conversations. It would be a class in which passion or wholeheartedness is facilitated. Its lessons would invite each person to express him- or herself freely while exploring the meaning of life and his or her place within the greater scheme of that life.

Young people are yearning for that sense of "place," for a rock to stand on and a way of being they can call their own. The term "peer pressure" is overused, and it has come to mean being pressured by others to do something. It is far more realistic and therefore authentic to speak of the pressure that comes from within in order to find a place of belonging without. Our students need and want to understand the many intricacies of the journey of life and how they can maneuver through the maze of external factors and events by using their sense of place, purpose, and passion as a grounding force, as a touchstone.

One way I seek to explain this is to draw two parallel lines on the board. These lines represent simultaneous lifelines of the group experience (the top or surface line) and the individual experience (the bottom or below-the-surface line). I state that the challenge is for the individual experience—the talents, interests, positions, and attitude of the person—to interface harmoniously with the group experience: what is accepted, what are the cultural norms, and what is embraced and celebrated.

If your individual "way" matches with the group "way," then you are all set. You are accepted and "in." For example, a guy who is a star football player in a school culture that values football would feel acceptance. If, on the other hand, your individual preference, talent, or way of life does not fall within the group norms, you are open to ridicule, scorn, or disinterest from the group. A good example of this might be a guy who studies ballet and attends the school that values football.

David Whyte's poem "The Journey" (1997, pp. 37–38) cuts to the core of the meaning of the challenges we encounter in our daily lives, particularly when we have had a major emotional setback. The poem reminds me as a teacher that in each new day I may play a part in helping my students look ahead to new beginnings with a stronger sense of courage and self.

The Journey

Above the mountains
the geese turn into
the light again

painting their
black silhouettes
on an open sky.

Sometimes everything
has to be
enscribed across
the heavens

so you can find
the one line
already written
inside you.

Sometimes it takes
a great sky
to find that

small, bright
and indescribable
wedge of freedom
in your own heart.

Sometimes with
the bones of the black
sticks left when the fire
has gone out

someone has written
something new
in the ashes
of your life.

You are not leaving
you are arriving.

—David Whyte,
The House of Belonging: Poems
(1997)

Real-Time Feedback

The poem "The Journey" emphasizes how important it is to be in "real-time" presence in each moment we experience:

> *You are not leaving*
>   *you are arriving.*

Real-time feedback, also known as in-the-moment feedback, is the most valid, authentic, and effective kind of feedback, whether one practices a violin and corrects one's fingering immediately in order to neurologically imprint the correction or stops everything the moment a child makes an inappropriate choice and has him or her role-play a more appropriate one. This is feedback at its finest because the purpose of feedback is to help the individual or group learn and grow from the information received. By delivering it without judgment and immediately, the opportunity for permanent change is greatly enhanced, almost as if the behavior change becomes a memory on the cellular level.

Real-time presence in teaching social skills relates to the exploration of a social situation that students experience every day as part of their daily rituals—in essence, "arriving" and noticing the moment the social situation is occurring. When teaching social skills, we are often helping students "un-learn" previous habits and cultivate new ones. When a child makes a mistake while reading aloud, we will ask him or her to stop and read the passage again. Similarly, when a student makes an anti-social choice, we must also freeze the moment and rewind the event by having the student think about the precipitating events and explore alternative responses. If we stop everything and have the people involved in the incident role-play the situation after being prompted with healthier choices, we are building new pathways of response and understanding within those students. This is how real-time feedback provides an opportunity for lasting change: by making a person more aware of the choices he or she has.

Speaking to students in real time through storytelling and reflection is exemplified by presenting the following scenario to a class:

> *Imagine you are with your friends and they're talking about a movie they've seen but you haven't. What would you say if someone turned to you and asked, "Have you seen it?" Would you say yes or no?*

Many will say, "I would just say I saw the movie."

When students are engaged in a courageous conversation, they reveal that they did not want to be left out. The intense need for connection is a universal desire, and all students know what it means to be left out and can imagine the feelings of another person who has been left out. The most effective social discovery lessons are facilitated as courageous conversations that invite real-time presence in which all students are encouraged to explore their thoughts, feelings, and ideas on a variety of social issues.

The Formula for Success

A social skills lesson has three strategies that create captivating lessons in which learning takes place:

- Make it real.

- Keep it simple.

- Make it memorable.

These strategies flow together to create the beginning, middle, and ending of a social skills lesson.

Strategy One: Make It Real

Some time ago I was preparing to teach a lesson on practicing empathy to a group of eighth-grade students. I had my guitar with me and before I even began, a brave girl came up to me and asked if I was going to sing "self-esteem sing-a-long feel-good songs." When I assured her I wasn't going to sing "Kumbaya," with a dramatic swipe of her brow she emphatically declared, "Well, that's a relief!" This amusing moment illustrated what kids need when learning a new social skill: they need to see that the lesson will be about something they can relate to, about things they experience each day. They do not need to be told what to do or that they should feel ashamed if they make a mistake.

This need for truth in a social skills lesson is best met through the sharing of real-life experiences and the memories and feelings associated with them. Your pool of material for this sharing can come from a variety of sources: your own stories and those of past students and friends. There is a certain mystique surrounding true stories, and we can maximize the appeal of these stories by using them to engage our students. Any lesson on relationships, friendship, choices, empathy, or compassion must focus on what is really going on through the eyes of the students. For example, ask your students, "Have you ever changed your clothes at least once before coming to school?" Most hands will go up. Continue by asking, "Who has ever had a parent or guardian select an article of clothing for you while shopping, and when the item was shown to you, you said something like, 'You can buy it, but I'm not gonna wear it'?" Most likely, this will elicit immediate laughter because most students will relate to the story. This opening conversation begins to identify the dynamics of what goes on between parents and students every day along with what influences the choices a student makes. In this case, the choice is what to wear or not to wear.

Once a connection has been established to the real-life event of what to wear, I ask the students, "What is so important about the clothes you wear?" In the next few minutes, the ideas that all people need to belong, have friends, be cool, or be accepted are presented, and students realize that most of the choices they make come from these needs. Awareness of this fact helps students understand why others do what they do: to fit in. This understanding is the first step of empathy: once a person can imagine and understand why someone thinks and feels a certain way, that person can act on these cognitive and emotional imaginings by moving into an empathic state.

Think of the familiar technique, for example, of a person who asks the therapist a sensitive and personal question "for a friend" as a safe way to ask a question for him- or herself. The opening to the conversation goes something like, "I have this friend who. . . ." It is always easier and safer to distance and separate oneself from a difficulty or challenge in one's life in order to gain an objective view of events.

You will know you are teaching a "real-life" lesson if a student says to you during the lesson, "It's like you're reading my mind. How do you know so much about what we go through?" You have made the material accessible, understandable, and safe. When I asked the eighth-grade girl who did not want to hear

"Kumbaya" what she and her classmates wanted from our lesson, she quickly replied, "Make it real life." She wanted something she and her classmates could relate to.

It is critical to teach the social lesson in real-life contexts—in ways in which the students can connect. Connecting means to open the students up to the significance of the particular skill you are teaching, often by telling a story, asking a series of questions about the meaning of the story, and encouraging them to share their own stories. For instance, I often introduce a lesson on the skill of listening by asking, "Who has ever been on the phone with someone and figured out that the person on the other end was watching television while you were talking to them?" I follow this question with, "How did it feel to know that someone was watching television when you were trying to tell them something? Why did you feel this way?"

When you engage your students by making the topics of the lesson real for them, you can move the lesson into the next phase or teaching strategy: keep it simple.

Strategy Two: Keep It Simple

Once you have stimulated interest in the lesson's social challenge or issue, you will need to break the desired social skill into its simplest components and name those components for the students. This process is called *naming the world*. In this context, naming the world means to apply names to life's challenging or difficult experiences as a way to process and understand cognitively what is happening during these experiences. The names we give to complicated social and emotional issues provide students with a common language for discussing and understanding the issues.

Two useful words I use to name the world of interpersonal dynamics are *connect* and *reject*. When I have made the lesson real for students and established the need everyone has to belong, I point out that when you break down interpersonal dynamics to its simplest form, we all have two choices to make each day: either reject (keep someone away or hurt them), or connect (welcome or seek to understand the person's story). I add that to connect does not necessarily mean to be someone's close friend. It means to honor the right all students have to feel safe in school and to be accepted for who they are.

I accompany these words with a visual that shows many small circles inside a large circle to symbolize *connect* and a separate, small circle off to the side to portray *reject:*

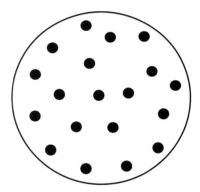

Choice of Connection   Choice of Rejection

The words "reject" and "connect" along with the diagram offer a clear, concise, and simple way of looking at the complexities of social decision making. It takes courage to leave the circle of connection to reach out to another, thus risking not being allowed to return to the circle of connection. I often sing or recite the words to the song "Courage" by Bob Blue to drive this point home. Here is an excerpt:

A small thing once happened at school
that brought up a question for me,
and somehow it taught me to see
the price that I pay to be cool.

Diane is a girl that I know.
She's strange like she doesn't belong.
I don't mean to say that that's wrong.
We don't like to be with her, though.

And so when we all made this plan
to have a big party at Sue's.
most kids in our school got the news,
but no one invited Diane.

The thing about Taft Junior High
is secrets don't last very long.
I acted like nothing was wrong
when I saw Diane start to cry.

—Bob Blue, Black Sox Music
(www.the-spa.com/bobblue1/)

(See page 206 for the complete lyrics to "Courage.")

When teaching or facilitating a lesson on a challenging social issue, I "spiral out" metaphorically or seek to use a universal symbol to which all can relate so that the students' interest is piqued, thereby opening them up to a significant learning experience. Most students will respond enthusiastically when asked to process the complexities of social decision making and will relate well to the idea of the "cartoon version" of one's conscience, in which a person has a little devil on one shoulder and a little angel on the other, both speaking to the person at the same time. Once the class has connected to this scenario, I tell them we all have two voices in our mind that exist in the form of simultaneous and conflicting thoughts. One voice whispers, "Do the right thing," while the other voice yells, "Do what you think others will think is cool." The question is: Which voice do you listen to, and which choice will you make?

If the strategy of keeping it simple has opened students up to sharing at this point, then the last strategy of the lesson—make it memorable—can be used.

Strategy Three: Make It Memorable

Making the lesson memorable is a combination of the first two teaching strategies previously mentioned. If the lesson is real and easily accessible, then it will be memorable. The strong emotions a student experiences in a social skills lesson become the glue that places the experience in the student's mind, making it stick there in the form of a strong emotional memory.

I often frame a lesson by declaring that if the students focus and give the experience a chance, they will have a memorable experience. I ask them what the word "emotion" means, and someone will say it has something to do with feelings. I add that an emotion can be a strong feeling and that when someone has a strong emotion (especially in the presence of others), that strong emotion will often become an emotional memory. I say, "If this lesson is 'real life,' then it will be memorable. There will be something you say or someone else says or a thought you may have during the course of this lesson that will become a lasting memory." We never know when we are going to have an emotionally memorable experience, but many emotional memories are tied to social issues—being teased in preschool, being retained in first grade, or being ridiculed in front of others in middle or high school, for example.

If the lesson is real life, if complex social situations are broken down to their simplest components, and if students are engaged and intrigued with what they are uncovering about their daily social challenges, then the lesson will be meaningful and memorable. If you close the lesson by asking students to complete a sentence summation or two such as, "One thing I learned is . . ." or "One thing that surprised me is . . . ," you will greatly enhance the chance for a memorable lesson that helps them rethink their choices. When someone verbalizes or, in some instances, declares a discovery in front of the entire group, the chances for that person learning the new skill and applying it will be strengthened. That is why declarations are such effective motivational tools.

Emotional Intelligence (EI)

In the book *Working With Emotional Intelligence* (1998), Daniel Goleman writes that "emotional intelligence refers to the capacity for recognizing our own feelings and those of others, for motivating ourselves, and managing emotions well in ourselves and in our relationships" (p. 317). When we think of students and our hope of impacting their social skills development in meaningful and positive ways, our initial step is to help them look inside at how they respond and act toward others, especially in times of stress—when they feel jealous about a friend, for example, or are meeting new people—and then reflect on how they develop and manage all of their relationships.

In Daniel Goleman, Richard Boyatzis, and Annie McKee's book *Primal Leadership: Learning to Lead with Emotional Intelligence* (2002), the authors offer an EI model with four domains: self-awareness, self-management, social awareness, and relationship management (p. 38). Empathy is identified as an emotional competence and one of the keys for being socially aware of others. To develop healthy, resilient, and emotionally satisfying relationships (both personally and professionally), social awareness and its accompanying behaviors must be strong. This includes having the ability to accurately read social situations and to be aware of the impact one's choices may have on others in any given moment. It is enlivening when a person can identify with another person. Thus, effectively teaching empathy as an EI competency is a sterling goal for the teacher who wishes to facilitate the present and future life success, achievement, and happiness of his or her students.

Emotional Literacy

Emotional literacy refers to a person's practical ability to apply his or her EI competencies in a way that builds helpful, caring, and empathic relationships—that is, to develop one's EI competencies to the point where they are accessible in one's daily interactions. This is especially crucial in times of stress when most people tend to respond through their emotions rather than through their rational thoughts. A person who is adept socially is essentially someone who can apply EI principles and has high EI competencies, whether the person is aware of them or not. Goleman further defines an EI competency as "a learned capability based on emotional intelligence that results in outstanding performance at work" (p. 25). I propose that a student with high emotional intelligence will have outstanding performance at school socially, emotionally, and academically.

The following list includes some of the emotional competencies identified by Goleman, Boyatzis, and McKee (2002, p. 39).

While the authors have identified empathy as a primary social awareness competency, I have chosen additional competencies from their list that apply to what I present in this book. I have also included communication from Dr. Goleman's earlier book *Working With Emotional Intelligence* (1998, p. 27).

1. Communication

2. Building bonds

3. Teamwork and collaboration

4. Leadership

5. Developing others

6. Conflict management

7. Influence

Communication

The three high-level listening responses of asking open-ended questions, clarifying and summarizing, and reflecting another's feelings accurately are the highest levels of communication and the most direct route to empathy. The greatest gift a person can offer to another is to be present and to listen, seeking to understand what that person is thinking and feeling. I have often shared the following equation with students: *Listening = I care.*

Teach your students to listen, and practice this exercise often. Whenever you have them work together, remind your groups to be mindful of their listening behaviors. Post the guidelines of an effective listener in your classroom and periodically refer to them (see page 91). When reviewing or preparing for a test, have your students practice their listening skills when they review the material together as partners or in small groups.

The Listening Wheel. The Listening Wheel is a process for teaching and practicing listening using two concentric circles. One group of students stands or sits as an inner circle facing out while a second group faces in. Each group takes turns answering questions that are provided by the teacher or group facilitator. While one group answers, the other group listens and asks open-ended questions to follow up on what they have heard. After a short period of time, perhaps 2 to 3 minutes, the facilitator stops the conversations, and the listeners tell their partners a summary of some of the information that was shared. After the summaries, the roles reverse. The circle that listened now answers questions from the other circle.

After each round, students in the outside circle move over two places to face new partners for new topics. This process helps the students practice their listening skills, involves everybody, and can be used as a fun way to review information from any subject area.

Here are some sample questions to set up the listening practice:

- What is your favorite time of day, and why?
- What is a recent success you have had?
- Where do you feel most comfortable, and why?
- What do you look for in a friend?
- Share a time when you helped another person.

Building Bonds

There is an art to making strong connections with others through compassionate and generous acts. Some time ago, I was helping a colleague facilitate his high school leadership training class when two girls—juniors in the class—told us they wanted to reach out to a boy who sat alone every day at lunch. They were unsure of how to do this. We suggested they ask if they could sit at the same table with this student as a first step to making a connection. They did this and eventually others joined in. One day the boy who was used to sitting alone showed up unexpectedly to a meeting of an after-school spirit club. Not only did he show up, but he also volunteered to take the lead in a school activity, and in time his entire school experience changed. All of this began with one little, yet very big act by two girls who were inspired to reach out to build a connection with another student.

Tell your students that when they take the initiative to talk to another person by practicing listening and showing an interest in that person, they will build a connection that will bring joy to both parties. One of the many benefits of generous and caring acts is that the giver receives just as much as the receiver.

Teamwork and Collaboration

Students who have the skills and group dynamics awareness to work effectively with others and thrive when doing so can often nurture other group members who are unsure of themselves. When the teacher provides group and cooperative opportunities, the skills necessary for understanding how others are feeling will be enhanced and strengthened.

When preparing your students to work in groups, first have them spend a lot of time working in pairs. It is much easier to work with one than with many, so this is the recommended place to start for group work training. The skills of listening, compromise, negotiation, support, and empathy are all improved by working with others.

Leadership

Leadership as it relates to empathy in this context is defined as maximizing the involvement of those you want to influence (Turney, 1994, p. 1). This often includes getting as much joy and satisfaction from another's achievements as from one's own, particularly if a person has contributed to another's success either by supporting or teaching that person or by setting up the circumstances in a situation for that person to succeed. This "behind-the-scenes" leadership approach is an empathic version of leadership that is reflective of a person who is emotionally healthy.

Peer leadership is my favorite of the many programs and groups I have been involved with in schools. Peer leadership trains students in communication, self-reflection, and planning skills. When the influence and power of students are harnessed in positive and helping ways, the culture change within a school will be evident and profound. The ideal scenario is for a school to create a leadership class for all students to take for either a semester or an entire school year. Leadership class should be considered to be as important as a study skills class because the leadership class provides a core set of life skills in the same way that a study skills class prepares students to achieve academically.

Developing Others

This competency focuses on the ability to see another person's talents and to nurture that person to see these talents and realize them fully. This ability requires selflessness and a great focus on and interest in the other person. In order to know a person's talents, especially if that person is unable to see them or unwilling to accept them, it is critical to focus on reading how that person responds to a variety of situations. This includes processing with a person after a particularly emotional event, such as an extreme disappointment or a significant achievement. Processing means to carry on a conversation with an individual in which he or she is able to articulate what happened, what he or she is thinking and feeling, and the next steps he or she will take. An example of a processing question is: "Have you thought about what you are going to do now?"

Peer mentoring programs are perfectly suited to provide the opportunity to apply this EI competency. When a student is trained in listening and offering helpful responses (two critical components of mentor training), empathy is a natural outcome.

Conflict Management

Students who have the pro-social skill of conflict management are capable of working through disagreements creatively. In fact, these students see a disagreement with another as an opportunity to create something new with that person while learning something about him- or herself. True empathic vision is when one can "see" things through another's eyes, paving the way for resolution, problem solving, and compassionate choices.

Consider teaching all of your students conflict management and a mediation process. Instill several common words into their language of conflict management such as "resolve," "choice," and "needs." Point out that conflict is natural: what is not natural is having the ability to overcome conflicts in healthy and productive ways. Gaining that ability is what conflict resolution or management is all about.

Peer mediation programs are a positive force when they work, but they must be cultivated with the necessary training and administrative, faculty, and parent support. An advisor must oversee the program to ensure consistency, and booster trainings must be provided to reinforce the program throughout the school year. When these steps are taken, mediation becomes a component of an empathic and caring culture.

Influence

People of influence are most effective when they treat others with honor and respect, especially those who are ostracized or are different from the group. When someone is influential with his or her peers, an individual choice by that person can become a group choice. Thus, when an influential person practices empathy, compassion, and caring for others, his or her peers will probably follow suit.

As an emotional competency, influence is an effective bullying prevention strategy because several studies show that in cases of bullying, peers were present approximately 85% of the time (Atlas & Pepler, 1998). "If just one bystander says 'stop,' or 'don't hit my friend,' the bully will stop half of the time" (Stossel, 2002).

Endeavor to provide "bystander training" that presents the dynamics of the bullying equation and highlights the significance of the bystanders. If the students adopt an empathic view and gain the necessary skills to communicate their concerns to fellow students, you will have taken them far in their journey to become positive influences.

Initiative

Empathy has to come from within for it to be most effective in practice. Self-motivated, caring young people often make social decisions based on wisdom and experience, not solely on what others (including adults) suggest or pressure them to do. You will see evidence that empathy is part of the culture when you notice students being nice to one another, working and talking together, and honoring and respecting each other. When these choices are self-motivated—when students take it upon themselves to support others without the prompting of a teacher—then you know that emotional safety is the norm within your school.

Feedback as Character Education (Influence)

When you notice students practicing any of the seven emotional competencies mentioned here, it is important to acknowledge their practice by expressing your appreciation through specific and direct feedback. Feedback is the most significant way to teach human dynamics in groups and relationships. Giving effective feedback is an art form—it is not criticism, judgment, or assertiveness. Instead, it is information for an individual, a group, or oneself. Feedback is observational, meaning that, in its purest form, it is given as what was said or heard and what was seen.

Here are two examples of observational feedback:

To an individual:

> "I want you to know how much I appreciated it when I saw you ask Susan to be in your study group. She had been sitting alone, and she smiled when you invited her in."

To a group:

> "Thanks for cleaning up the classroom after our party. There was garbage all over the floor, and

without my asking, about 10 of you picked up the garbage, put it in the trash, and swept the floor. It really made it easier for me later in the day. Again, thanks to all who helped."

Sincere appreciation for specific empathic acts goes a lot further than posters in the hallway, daily character education quips read over the PA system, or one-time flashy assemblies. While these strategies can prove effective, they must be seen as part of a comprehensive initiative.

Emotional safety within our schools is just as critical as physical safety, and it must be given the same level of importance. Just as we would not implement only some safety strategies and not others—having a single point of entry on Mondays and Tuesdays, for example—we must also seek to implement a coordinated and complete set of social and emotional programmatic strategies. In a sense, the single point of entry for this area of concentration is through the heart, and we must approach this challenge with vigilance, focus, and consistency.

Cross Training and Rituals

When you are teaching pro-social skills, differentiate the lessons by using a variety of approaches and techniques. This will make the lessons more novel and interesting and will also help you meet the diverse learning needs of your students. If you spend time each day teaching a pro-social skill strategy, you will begin to create a sense of ritual and ceremony regarding the significance of the skill building you are facilitating. Author Laura Day writes about rituals in her book, *The Circle: How the Power of a Single Wish Can Change Your Life* (2001):

A ritual is any act performed in a ceremonial or intentional way, usually on special occasions or on a recurring basis. . . . We can use them to acknowledge the profound importance of anything. . . . Rituals are important because we invest them with meaning. (p. 40)

Rituals do not have to be specific lessons. They can be reminders for students to apply social skills as they work in your classroom. Although one's way of "being" (social modeling) can be ritualized, consistency, focus, and compassion are the key to its effectiveness. The greatest challenge for me in working with educators and future teachers is to clearly make the distinction between process (the how) and content (the what). Here is a simple way to express this difference:

If you are watching a group of students who are working together and close your eyes, <u>what you hear is the content</u>. If you open your eyes and cover your ears, <u>what you see is the process</u>.

The following empathy-building *processes* can be used to teach the *content* of your subject matter.

- Power of Two (partner sharing)
- Small group work
- Role playing
- Large group conversation and exploration
- Journal writing
- Poetry and songwriting
- Definitions

The Power of Two

I learned the phrase "power of two" from my friend and colleague, Robert Greenleaf (1998). There could not be a more accurate descriptor for partner sharing (p. 2). When two people work together on a task or challenge and practice a variety of social skills, the creativity of two combined becomes a powerful force indeed.

Once certain basics are taught—such as listening, negotiating, and compromising—you can have students work in pairs while prompting them to keep their social skills in mind. In time you will no longer need to remind them as the practice of honor in collaboration becomes the norm. When this happens, you are ready to move the students into working cooperatively in groups.

Small Group Work

Cooperative learning requires students to have a high degree of emotional intelligence if they are to work effectively with other group members. People often say that they train students in consensus as their group process, when in fact consensus is not a process but rather an outcome. An example of a *process* is a planning procedure that has been chosen by the teacher. Whatever the process, if a group is to work effectively enough to reach consensus, all members must be involved and each person's ideas must be honored.

It takes time to train young people to work well together, but it certainly is worth the effort. Students will learn about the importance of seeking to understand another person's viewpoint (a form of empathy), and they will learn about their own behavior in groups.

When your students are comfortable with the group process, you can integrate this approach from time to time into your lessons. The appendix in this resource includes SNAP—a student, consensus-building planning process on page 198 that incorporates many of the pro-social skills described in this section.

Role Playing

Role playing provides the opportunity for students to safely act out new skills in typically challenging social situations. I have found that role playing acts as an emotional hook that helps students explore challenging social situations in which a tough decision must be made (such as going against what others are saying or doing). The role play helps the student experience the social situation being portrayed.

Teacher-Led

In the beginning two to three teachers or staff members act out a social situation. For example, two kids gossip about another kid and a third joins in. The modeling of a social situation by the adults also models role playing and risk taking, thereby opening up more students to role playing themselves. Once the teachers finish the initial role play, they ask the class questions about what was presented and elicit alternative choices that could have been made. After a few alternative choices are offered, the role players reenact the situation using the suggestion made by students and in the process change the outcome.

Role-Play Rewind

If two students are in the middle of a conflict over something one student did to the other, dialogue about what happened and what could have been done differently. Then have the two students "rewind" back to the event and immediately put into practice the alternative choice that was identified.

Large Group Conversation and Exploration

In order to lead a large group conversation effectively, the teacher takes on the role of facilitator. If the lesson is conducted as a collective exploration rather than as a lecture on right or wrong, then it is a conversation. This approach is particularly appropriate for lessons on empathy and other pro-social skills and behaviors.

The key to effective large group conversations lies in the use of facilitative responses. According to author and educator Tom Turney (1994), the highest levels of facilitative responses are:

1. Reflecting feelings

2. Asking open-ended questions (beginning with who, what, where, how, and when)

3. Clarifying and summarizing (pp. 55–60)

Here is a typical sequence of large group conversation questions that can be used to introduce the notion of learning social skills:

1. What does it mean to have a skill?

2. What is a skill you have?

3. How can you improve your skill level in something?

4. What is a social skill?

5. When is it necessary to have social skills?

6. Where in your life do you use them?

7. What are some social skills you feel are important? (Use this question in a brainstorming activity.)

This set of questions takes an entire period or two to process and learn from. The critical skill as the facilitator is to ask an appropriate follow-up question for each student response and then to summarize what has been offered. This is more challenging than it may seem, but over time you will find yourself flowing with a group of students as you explore a variety of social issues together.

Journal Writing

Journaling provides students with a mechanism for refined reflection. Once a person is in the "journaling mode," he or she is thinking internally and going deeper into a lesson. Author Marianne Williamson (1997) once said "the deeper one travels inward the further outward that person will travel." I take traveling outward to mean helping to make positive change in the world. A first step toward this is to reach out to others in an effort to help and support them in hopes of making a difference in their lives. Journaling in its many forms is the first step in Marianne Williamson's equation: traveling inward. What follows are some examples of journaling techniques.

Letters

Have students write letters to a person they have read about in a story, poem, or song. Here is a student letter written to Howard Gray, a person in a song who has been unfairly treated:

Dear Howard,

We listened to the song about you. It was very touching. It made me realize how much it hurts to get picked on. Sometimes I pick on people that don't have cool clothes. I never really realized that maybe I was hurting their feelings. I don't think I have ever really wanted to hurt someone but now that I think about it, maybe I have without even realizing it.

I'm not fat now, actually I was never fat but when I was in third or fourth grade I had a friend that always told me I was. I was a little chubby but when I grew I thinned out. But now, no matter how many people tell me I look good and no matter how many guys ask me out, I still don't think I'm trim enough. All this because I was teased in third grade. I wish teasing could just stop, I don't know how but I wish it could. Everyone would be much happier and our world would be a much better place. It's unbelievable how cruel kids can be sometimes and the scars of it can last a lifetime.

—*Carrie, an eighth-grade student*

(For a description of a lesson using the song "Howard Gray," see section 4, page 126.)

Imaginative Role Reversals

After exploring the lives of people from around the globe, students write a journal entry in which they imagine they are another person living in another place far away. This is particularly effective and moving when the activity is relevant to contemporary issues or when it complements study of a part of the globe in which the culture and/or the living conditions are drastically different. As empathy becomes more ingrained into a person, it becomes part of the thought process of understanding human rights issues all over the world, thus providing an opportunity to live out the truism expressed by Mohandas Gandhi (2003): *You must be the change you wish to see in the world.*

Poetry and Songwriting

Poet and anthologist Naomi Shihab Nye has edited two wonderful books of poetry by poets from other parts of the world:

- *The Same Sky: A Collection of Poems From Around the World* (1992)

- *The Space Between Our Footsteps: Poems and Paintings From the Middle East* (1998)

Her books serve as examples of how stories, poems, songs, and paintings about and by others can be used to begin a class dialogue about differences, understanding, and the human condition. The activity continues as an empathy writing assignment in which students take on the thoughts and feelings of another. I encourage you to explore these anthologies for poems you could share with your students. One possible selection is "The Train of the Stars" by Abdul-Raheem Saleh Al-Raheem, a poet from Iraq (translated by Adil Saleh Abid). His poem appears on page 37 of *The Space Between Our Footsteps* (Nye, 1998).

Al-Raheem likens the night to a train that is passing, a train that carries all of the things a night can have:

> . . . moons and stars
> Clouds, flowers,
> Seas and rivers that run.

The poet finds himself wishing he could take this train one day:

> To see where it's going.
> Oh, where's that train going?

If you chose to read the entire poem to your students, its meaning could be explored through a class dialogue. Some questions might include:

1. How is the night like a train?

2. Where does the night travel?

3. Do you feel that the poet longs to be somewhere else? Explain your answer.

4. What do *you* imagine as you look into the night sky?

After a class dialogue, students may write their own poems about something they think, feel, or long for as they look into the night sky or as they spend time in their own "night sky" of reflection.

I often write songs with a class or teach the process so that individuals or small "songwriting teams" can write as well. One goal is to demystify this form of expression while nurturing individual expression of how students see their daily social interactions. To have your students engage in songwriting, present the following ideas to them:

1. Songwriting is an act of translating real-life experiences.

2. Songwriting is a craft and can be learned.

3. You can build on the writing skills you already have when you write songs.

The following songwriting process can be used to guide your students:

Write the Lyrics

1. Ask students to write a first line to a song (anything that comes to them).

2. Invite some students to read their lines aloud to the class.

3. Divide students into groups of four.

4. Have each group use some of the lines and work together to write one verse and one chorus.

5. Have members of each group share what they have written.

Put the Lyrics to Music

6. To do this, I like to let the students choose the style of music for their songs, and this choice leads to the creation of the melody. Play some recorded samples of different types of music: the blues, rock, or country. Also consider offering the choice of tempo as slow, moderate, or fast.

   Then have them explore reading their lyrics aloud in a rhythmic fashion. The rhythm alone could give them their melody or "feel." I have had students perform their lyrics in a rap form. However you facilitate the process and whatever their choices, the important thing is to allow the melody to come from them with a little guidance from you.

   You could extend this activity by having students record their songs or write and then teach a reflection lesson to accompany their songs.

Optional Activity

Consider having your student create "zipper songs." These songs use the music from a familiar song. Students "zip" out one group of words from the song and "zip" in new words they have created.

Here is a sample set of lyrics written by a student in a song-writing session I conducted:

> I lost a friend.
> Will he ever forgive me again?
> I regret it now.
> Forgive me,
> forgive me somehow.
>
> I made fun of him,
> and I called him some names.
> I guess he didn't,
> Didn't think it was a game,
> Didn't think it was a game.

Definitions

Have students write their own definitions of ideas that have been covered. Some of these might include *empathy, compassion, optimism, courage,* and *perseverance.* After writing these down, students share what they have written with the class. This exercise is not intended as a quiz or test, but rather it is a reflection experience in which students identify what these concepts mean to them.

The Class Meeting

The empathic process begins with an individual's perspective of a situation and spirals out from there. In the book *Seven Arrows* (1972), the author Hyemeyohsts Storm tells of the significance of the circle and the connectedness we have to everyone and everything. He points out that if a group of people is sitting together in a circle and an object is placed in the center, each person would have a unique perspective of what the object looked like. This indicates how complicated situations can be when there is more than one person involved. In order to understand, relate to, and connect with other people's unique perspectives, one must be open and flexible to their viewpoints and experiences (p. 4).

The circle is the most connecting symbol there is in the Native American tradition. This connecting circle provides a profound symbol for the healing or wholeness which comes from being a member of a group, class, or school in which empathy and other compassionate behaviors are practiced. In the classroom the connecting circle is the class meeting. In the words of Eric Schaps (2002), director of the Developmental Studies Center, "the class meeting is the most underutilized process there is in the classroom today."

The purpose of the class meeting is to provide an open forum in which class members can share their thoughts, feelings, or ideas about class issues. The process has students seated in a circle, preferably not behind desks. Students do not have to raise their hands to speak but rather wait until there is an opening in the action to share something with the group. After a person speaks, someone else may respond to what has been said or they may offer a new and unique view. Not everyone has to speak, but all must listen to what is being said.

After the meeting has been closed by the teacher, a summary is provided. The summary can relate to the content, such as, "Today many people spoke of how nervous they feel about next week's testing," or the summary can relate to the process, such as, "The meeting today was quiet because only six people spoke. Most of you were looking down and some had your arms crossed." Process statements can be more valuable than content statements because they often capture the subtle essence of what people in the group are feeling and sensing. Unless the expression of feelings by students in your class is encouraged, the meeting may never get below the surface to what is really going on with your class.

Over time, you can train students to summarize class meetings as they refine their own processing skills. The ability to process is one of the great empathic skills we can provide for our students. Processing requires one to be intent on the feelings of a person, a group, or an emotionally charged situation—this intent, or focus, is primary for empathic practice.

The class meeting can serve many purposes, ranging from the general, such as checking in to see how everyone is doing, to the specific, as in "Let's talk about next week's math test." The value of a meeting is that it is a ritual in which all people can speak and be heard. Class meetings require a variety of pro-social skills. The teacher is truly a facilitator who opens and closes the meeting and allows the class or group to take responsibility for what occurs during the meeting. Regular class meetings help create a strong sense of community within the group. In fact, I used to call the meetings in my classroom "community meetings."

A class meeting has three primary rules:

1. One person speaks at a time.

2. No side conversations.

3. Honor everyone's point of view.

After you review the rules and clarify what they mean, you have the opportunity to weave in additional insights on empathy. This is just one example of how empathy education can be an integrative process in everything we do. Here is how I present the class meeting rules:

One person speaks at a time: When someone is speaking it is critical to focus on that person. If more than one person is speaking, we are not listening but competing for "airtime." Everyone will have a chance to share his or her views. It is critical to wait your turn and listen to each person as they speak.

No side conversations: We want to hear from each of you. If you share only with the person next to you, we miss out and it distracts others in the group, including the person who is listening to you.

Honor everyone's point of view: Honor in this context means not to judge others but rather to seek to understand where they are coming from. When people judge or label, they are often mistaken and never really get a chance to know and understand the other person.

Three Types of Class Meetings

Focused. In a focused class meeting, the teacher presents the group with a focused issue or question with the goal of having the group analyze the situation, make a decision, or both. All community members are invited to express their questions, concerns, or suggestions about the issue or task at hand. Each time one person shares, the rest of the group listens for understanding.

Open. An open meeting provides a forum in which students can express their thoughts, feelings, or ideas about any issue or issues they wish to address. These can range from concerns about a subject area to challenges with interpersonal situations in the classroom or school. Students may also share exciting or prideful news as well as something specific that they have created, such as artwork, a piece of music, or an essay. The purpose is to give everyone the opportunity to speak and be heard in a caring and structured way.

The morning meeting. The Northeast Foundation for Children uses the Morning Meeting as part of its Responsive Classroom Process (www.responsiveclassroom.org/about/aboutnefc.html). The Morning Meeting has a specific purpose and flow of events. It is used exclusively first thing in the school day, and it follows this sequence:

1. A greeting (for example, a good morning and a high five passed around the circle)

2. A sharing followed by questions and comments

3. A group activity to be completed by the entire class

4. News and announcements: logistics covered for the day

The Morning Meeting is an important example of a classroom ritual which helps ground the students in a new day and facilitates the practice of social skills and group building. For more on the Morning Meeting, see *The Morning Meeting Book* (2002) by Roxann Kriete in the Additional Resources.

The Fishbowl

Empathy in practice begins by honoring another person's experience. The fishbowl activity provides an opportunity to do this. A fishbowl presents the students with a unique perspective for learning something new or talking about something difficult while practicing a multitude of social skills, such as listening, processing, negotiating, giving feedback, receiving feedback, planning with others, and resolving conflicts or disagreements.

Begin this activity by having your entire class seated in a circle. Place five to six empty chairs in the center, thus creating a small empty circle within a larger circle. Provide the class with a topic and introduce it by saying, "Today we will explore the difficulties in working with others during a cooperative learning lesson."

Ask for volunteers to come into the center—these people are the "fish" that will interact in the center. The role of the students in the outer circle is to observe and listen to what happens among the fish and then provide feedback at the designated time.

The Fish

The fish are given the task of having a conversation with one another based on the topic. The standard approach is to focus on a topic or issue relevant to what is going on in the class socially or academically. The issue is presented as two related questions with each question presented one at a time over two rounds. Here are two questions that work well with a fishbowl:

Round One:

1. What are some of the concerns people have about next week's testing?

Round Two:

2. What are some ways to overcome these concerns?

The first question is posed for the fish, and once each person indicates he or she understands the question, the fishbowl is "opened" by the teacher. At this point, the fish begin talking about the question while people on the outside "bowl" listen and take notes. The teacher pays close attention to the fish and may stop them for any of the following reasons:

- There seems to be a natural break.

- The fish seem stymied and do not know what to say.

- The fish have gotten off task and are not addressing the question or issue that was raised.

After the first round (question one), the outside students (the bowl) are asked for feedback on the process.

The Bowl

The students in the larger circle have the same perspective as a person who is looking into a fish tank—seeing but not interacting directly with the fish. Once the inside circle has been "frozen," as when the teacher says, "I'm going to freeze the fish now," the outside circle is asked for feedback: "What did you hear and what did you see?"

Class members are encouraged to provide feedback on content (what was said) as well as on process (how the fish were interacting).

Here are some sample content feedback statements:

- "The group talked about the stress of next week's testing."

- "David indicated that his sister was helping him study."

- "Sandy questioned why we had to take these tests in the first place."

Here are some sample process feedback statements:

- "At first the group was quiet and everyone was looking down."
- "I counted six interruptions and two multiple conversations."
- "I noticed that Adrienne didn't speak one time."

The purpose of the process feedback is to offer information that will help the inside group be more productive as they continue their conversation. The skills of noting behaviors and delivering feedback in a nonjudgmental way that is free of labels reflect a high skill level of communication and empathy. Even when students deliver feedback without judgment, the person receiving it may take it as criticism. Therefore, it is also a skill to receive feedback in the spirit with which it is offered: to help a person grow.

Feedback is practiced every time you run a fishbowl. After the outside circle has delivered its feedback, the second question is asked and the fishbowl continues.

The second question is intended to move the fish toward closure or decision making. After exploring the first question and then receiving feedback from the outside, the fish are ready to focus on solutions.

After the second round, the fish are frozen, additional feedback is provided, and the fish are given 2 to 3 minutes to share any final thoughts with their fellow fish. At the very close of the fishbowl always thank the fish and express your appreciation for their involvement, acknowledging that their role was a challenging one.

Once the bowl has been closed, the inner circle folds into the outer circle to form one large circle, and the class comes together in a class meeting to talk about any issues that came up during the fishbowl.

The Empty Chair Variation: Vary the second round of the fishbowl by introducing an empty chair. After round one has been completed, place an additional chair in the center before opening the fishbowl up for round two. This empty chair is available for anyone from the outside who wishes to offer an insight or ask a question.

When a person leaves the outer circle and sits in the empty chair, he or she must wait to be recognized by one of the fish. Sitting in the empty chair does not mean that a person becomes a fish. It means that person is a visitor. After making his or her point, that person must return to his or her place in the outside circle. The fish can choose whether or not they will respond to what was offered.

Purposes of the Fishbowl
The fishbowl can be used for any of the following purposes:

- Resolving conflicts (the disputants become the fish)
- Planning
- Reviewing what has been learned
- Exploring classroom issues

- Practicing listening skills, note-taking skills, and speaking skills

Gender fishbowl: Have the fish be all of the girls in the class with the boys in the outer circle for one round and then flip-flop and then have the boys and girls change roles for the second round. You can use this approach when seeking to provide perspectives on an issue which that might be seen differently by both genders.

Group emissary fishbowl: Divide the class into small groups that are each given a task (interpreting a reading passage, for example). After the task has been completed, ask each group to send one student into the bowl to present his or her group's position. The rest of the group members make up the outside "bowl." After one round, each fish returns to his or her group to receive "coaching" from group mates. You may also create a tag team approach in which any group member may tag an inner fish to trade places. This allows group members to substitute for a group member and enter the fishbowl "on the fly" to introduce an additional thought or idea inside the bowl.

Because a fishbowl by design separates students in a classroom into two distinct roles, it is critical to end each fishbowl session with a group class meeting to process the information and reconnect the entire group.

Authenticity, Empathy, and Personal Growth

I feel such joy when I look into the sparkling eyes of a student who is completely enraptured with a conversation about life's many experiences and about how most of those experiences are universal. A good story is the best possible "hook" there can be when you want to engage a group of learners during a social discovery session. Sometimes, the energy bubbles over, and you will need to introduce a talking stick or a tennis ball that is tossed to whomever wishes to speak without interruption. Teaching and learning empathy can be a peak experience when the setting is safe enough to invite all involved to drop their defenses and become genuinely interested and involved. When this authenticity is present, vulnerability and personal growth will occur.

Although the choice of empathy—and therefore personal growth—starts from within, it must be cultivated from without. The school must intentionally create and coordinate the conditions for empathy, compassion, courage and understanding. When it does, it is ready to take the next step and become a School of Belonging, a place where all people feel welcomed, supported, and cared for. The next section provides guidance on how you can help your entire school become a place of belonging.

An effective listener . . .

1. Makes and keeps eye contact

2. Has good listening posture

3. Asks open-ended questions

4. Clarifies and summarizes

5. Reflects partner's feelings

Section 3

Living Empathy: The School of Belonging

Help us to be the always hopeful
Gardeners of the Spirit
Who know that without darkness
Nothing comes to birth
As without light
Nothing flowers.

—May Sarton (1971, p. 23), Poet and Writer

Agents of Change

A school of belonging is the articulation of an emotionally safe social culture within a school. It is not a program but rather the result of a series of intentions that are inclusive, needs-focused, and skill-based—intentions that create an environment that is secure, predictable, collaborative, and caring. This section describes what such an environment might look and feel like.

A Tale of Two Meetings

Two meetings with different schools provide examples of the absence and presence of qualities that create a School of Belonging. I was recently invited to join a friend who was facilitating a meeting with staff from an alternative school for middle and high school students. The group included teachers, learning assistants, crisis workers, and administrators. A community meeting format was used to collectively assess the status of a variety of school improvement plans that had been developed earlier in the school year.

The variety of plans included efforts to revamp the behavior system, simplify the code of conduct, and improve the school climate as a whole. As each spokesperson of the planning groups reported on the plans in frustrating tones and with angst, the energy level in the room became heavier and heavier. Within 70 minutes, the meeting had become a complaint session about the behaviors of kids and the lack of support to deal with these behaviors. No one was immune from blame: the parents, the police, the community, the media, and society as a whole. The longer the meeting continued, the stronger the feelings of hopelessness and frustration within the group became. Without naming it, the group was projecting the primary issue: they worked in an emotionally unsafe school. As I sat there listening, I felt the energy drain out of me.

Three days later, I facilitated a group of social workers from a different school district. Each person represented one of seven elementary schools in the district and shared thoughts about projects that had been launched in his or her schools since the school year began. The many topics discussed ranged from training a cadre of fifth graders to be referee "leaders" to reduce arguments during recess to creating a "Bully Buster" mailbox where students could anonymously ask for help for themselves or others (a low-risk bystander intervention strategy).

As each person shared, the energy in the room became lighter and lighter—inspired, one might say. People took notes and enthusiastically asked questions to learn more about the various programs and projects. This meeting focused on programs that met the needs of the students in their schools. The feeling within the group most likely reflected the same feelings that many of the students in their schools felt each day: ones of safety, inspiration, and motivation.

The feelings of the social culture within a school are evoked by the energy of all the people who spend time there: the teachers, students, other staff members, and the parents. When a culture is positive and authentic, this positive and authentic energy will be felt in most interactions that take place during the school day.

Connection Through Relationships

In a School of Belonging, the fundamental belief is that all members of the school population deserve to feel connected through the cultivation of helpful and positive relationships. A

School of Belonging establishes a system of feedback that is natural, integrated, and connecting. Daily academic and social stressors will be managed effectively when people are conscious of their thoughts, actions, and words about and toward others and when they are given opportunities to help others and build bonds of acceptance instead of barriers of rejection. This will result in a safer, more productive school where everyone is working together toward a unified goal of trust and emotional safety.

The Basic Premises for the School of Belonging

In a School of Belonging, connectedness is a critical first step. When people feel a sense of connection to one another, a unified vision for what it takes to build a school of belonging will take shape. The following characteristics form the basis of a School of Belonging:

- The School of Belonging requires a concerted effort, high skill level, and caring intentions on the part of all staff members.

- The social and emotional needs of all students are honored.

- Any form of emotional violence is entirely unacceptable.

- Staff and students participate in regular focus groups. This helps the school personnel keep current on the emotional dynamics of the school while providing students with a sense of collaboration.

- Cultural literacy initiatives are coordinated and in harmony with social and emotional learning initiatives (for example, empathy and diversity training).

- Teachers are provided with a structure that allows them to act as reflective practitioners. This means time is provided for teachers to meet with colleagues to process how they are doing and to share successes and frustrations.

The 10 Intentions

An intention is a focused thought to bring about the conditions a person wants. Once an intention is articulated and expected, its presence will be felt, even in the most subtle of forms. The following 10 intentions that create a School of Belonging are felt through specific practices, programs, and activities.

1. **The presence of a supportive leader.** This person is child oriented, is an effective listener, provides staff with numerous opportunities to work collaboratively, encourages innovative efforts, and is available to those who wish to speak with him or her.

2. **Effective social and emotional in-service training.** This involves carefully planned, high-quality, and relevant learning experiences for teachers, other professional staff, teaching assistants, monitors, and bus drivers. Training should include follow-up assistance and implementation materials (books, videos, DVDs, or lesson plans) for those who are interested in integrating social and emotional learning into their curriculum areas. This intention includes encouraging professional staff to meet in book clubs to discuss current educational literature and materials.

3. **An inviting school office.** Anyone who comes into the school or calls on the phone feels welcome by the office staff.

4. **Assembly programs or student workshops.** Programs for students are thoughtful and well organized. Teachers receive support materials (discussion questions, writing prompts, and lessons) before and after the assembly.

5. **Mentor programs for staff and students.** These programs focus on academic and social needs as well as on transition issues, such as incoming middle school students or a new student from another community.

6. **Monthly grade-level community meetings** are facilitated for students, giving them the opportunity to speak about important issues with their peers and classroom teachers. Smaller schools can hold an all-school monthly community meeting. Some schools have daily morning sings in which the musical experience and messages of the songs strengthen the sense of a caring community.

7. **Daily celebration and recognition of students.** Students are celebrated and recognized each day for a variety of reasons but most significantly as a way to help each person realize his or her unique gift or talent.

8. **A variety of extracurricular activities for all students.** Activities beyond athletics are offered, and students are encouraged to participate in the activities that interest them.

9. **Alternative programming** is provided for students who have different social, emotional, and academic needs.

10. **Parent workshops** are provided in ways that are inclusive and focus on critical issues.

Intention 1: The Presence of a Supportive Leader

The leadership of a school is a critical influence on the school's culture and climate. Principals must be able to articulate their vision for their schools and encourage staff to dialogue with them about education and the learning needs of the students. Indeed, all staff members must have input into the mission of the school along with its guiding principles and behavioral guidelines. In *Professional Learning Communities at Work* (1998), Richard DuFour and Robert Eaker describe the following benefits of establishing a clear, shared vision:

1. Shared vision motivates and energizes people.

2. Shared vision creates a proactive orientation.

3 Shared vision gives direction to people within the organization.

4. Shared vision establishes specific standards of excellence.

5. Shared vision creates a clear agenda for action. (p. 84)

Leaders must also be aware of their emotional tendencies during trying and stressful times and seek to manage those tendencies if they are counterproductive, making an effort instead to move on to healthy collaborative relationships. Leaders must be available, be visible, and actively seek to establish and maintain healthy and productive professional relationships.

Leaders have to be authentic and ask for help without being afraid of appearing weak. The best way to get people to work with you is to ask for their help or input. A leader has to be human and authentic, able and willing to communicate what he or she is truly thinking and feeling to those (the staff and parents) with whom he or she is working.

Intention 2: Effective Social and Emotional In-Service Training

Teachers and other staff must be presented with the most up-to-date training, and the administration must show commitment to any training initiative. I have been involved in many in-service trainings as the facilitator or presenter. At some of these events, unfortunately, the principal introduced me and then made a rapid exit when the workshop began. People always notice when the administrator leaves and does not participate. The administrator's departure leaves the impression that he or she thinks that the training is unnecessary or that he or she has better things to do.

The administrator must know what the workshop or training is about and must also have direct involvement or input into what will be provided for the teachers. I recommend that the school or district send a representative to an in-service offering in a neighboring district or at a conference to determine if the material and its presentation are appropriate for those who will experience the training or workshop session in their school. It also should complement any on-going system initiatives. For example, I am working with one district that has been working in-depth for 2 years on cultural literacy for its staff. My role has been to augment this effort by working with staff and students on a pro-culture building initiative that focuses on emotional safety and bullying prevention. Empathy education has proven to be an effective bridge between these initiatives.

In-service training is viewed unfavorably—and often referred to as the "flavor of the month"—when it is just an add-on or a "one-time offering" simply to accommodate a department of education mandate or to fill a day that has been set aside for staff development by the school district.

Any of the following in-service topics will have relevance to a school's efforts to teach empathy and create a School of Belonging:

- Diversity awareness/cultural literacy
- Active listening and facilitative feedback (de-escalation)
- Emotional intelligence (EI)
- Mentoring and its effects
- Social skills training
- Mediation and conflict management programs
- Student leadership programs
- Classroom management and community building
- Differentiated instruction
- Tolerance education

Intention 3: An Inviting Front Office

The front office is the hub of the school where people come and go, phones ring, announcements are made, and paperwork is handled. This busyness can get in the way of focused, caring interactions. The front office must be a safe harbor where students are comfortable and feel like they belong. Too often, I have seen students walk into the office to use the phone, for example, and feel like intruders rather than members of a school community.

When a student, parent, or other visitor enters the office, it is best to greet that person immediately in a positive way. The office personnel who receive interpersonal training with an EI (emotional intelligence) focus and practice what they learn will be huge assets to the climate of the office. For many people, the initial impression they have of a school is a lasting one and is often created by their first front office experience, whether in person or on the telephone.

Intention 4: Assembly Programs or Student Workshops

Ideally, assembly offerings for students are enlivening, entertaining, and thought-provoking. Even when this is so, the lasting effects of an assembly will only be as meaningful as the support materials that are provided. I highly recommend that schools hold a staff in-service before the assembly. I have often seen a class show up for an assembly with no pre-set notions and with many of the students thinking, "This is great. We don't have class today!"

An assembly should be more than the fulfillment of a PTO budget item or a "nice break for the kids." Any alternative offering such as an assembly must complement and reinforce the culture of the school, being consistent with the best guiding principles that have been set forth and modeled. Those who plan assembly programs should investigate the quality and meaningfulness of the speakers, performers, or entertainers. Assemblies that are fun, emotional, and thought-provoking can make a lasting impression on the students or, at the very least, provide the faculty with opportunities for follow up.

Intention 5: Mentor Programs for Staff and Students

Mentor programs are one of the most critical aspects of a School of Belonging because the person who receives the mentor's support is provided with a sense of grounding by someone who becomes a significant person in their lives. Here are three types of mentor programs:

- Teacher to teacher

- Adult to student

- Student to student

Teacher to teacher. This process pairs an experienced teacher with a first- or second-year teacher. Some programs also pair substitute teachers with a mentor. The role a mentor serves for a less-experienced colleague is to offer support, information, and encouragement. A mentor is trained in listening and feedback skills. One effective training method is to give mentors and protégés an opportunity to plan together how their mentoring relationship will work. For example, a mentor and protégé might review their guidelines together, decide how often they will connect during the week, and determine the time and purpose of their meetings. The protégés appreciate having someone to talk to, lean on, and sometimes commiserate with.

First-time mentors are often surprised that they receive as much from the relationship as the person they are mentoring. As it turns out, much can be learned from someone who has a fresh perspective, almost an innocence of hope and optimism that can be contagious. The greatest gift to give oneself is to give *of* oneself—to give is to truly receive. In mentoring, everyone involved receives a wealth of positive feelings and growth experiences.

Adult to student. In this kind of mentoring, any adult in the school who wants to be a mentor is trained to understand the needs of students and active listening skills, with an emphasis on what a mentor is (basically a supportive adult who cares) and is not (a best friend or substitute family member). Mentors can be teachers, teaching assistants, the principal or assistant principal, a custodian, and any other interested adult who can touch the life of a child and is willing to be trained.

Each mentor is assigned to a student. All mentors and their students meet together at the beginning to be introduced to the program and to have initial time to work together in pairs to plan how to connect in some way each day, if that is possible. The only limit placed on who is paired with whom is the recommendation that teachers do not mentor any of their current students. Sometimes a person will mentor a student for more than 1 year. The bond that is created can have a profound positive impact on the lives of both the mentor and the protégé.

Student to student. One year, a local school serving grades 7-12 had more middle school students in need of adult mentors than the number of adults available to serve them. To meet the need, a cadre of high school students in grades 11 and 12 were trained to act as mentors and then paired with an incoming seventh-grade student. Each pair of students then had a number of shared communication days in which the pair wrote its plan for working together. The school's homerooms were set up so that all mentors had a shared homeroom with their seventh-grade protégés. This assured them of connecting at least once each day. This program is still going strong today, 15 years after it began.

As in all generous acts, both parties gain from the mentoring relationship and in the process develop a greater sense of empathy and compassion for each other. Many of the relationships in any mentor program often continue beyond the school year and can still be viable many years later.

Intention 6: Monthly Grade Level Community Meetings

Lawrence Kohlberg and colleagues (Kohlberg, Lieberman, Higgins, & Power, 1981) espoused the democratic process in schools through what he referred to as Just Community Schools. In these schools, all people have the opportunity to speak and be heard and fairness and the rights of all are the primary focus. Foremost in this process is the class meeting described in section 2 on page 80. A school can set up its own version of a just community by conducting monthly grade-level community meetings. A strong bond to each other and the school itself is created when all students meet in a monthly ritual to speak in an open forum about ideas, thoughts, concerns, appreciations, and celebrations. Some students may be reluctant at first, but once this social and emotional ritual is established, everyone will be eager for the meetings to occur because they provide the opportunity to connect with others in a safe way.

If classes periodically hold class meetings, the grade-level community meeting will flow more easily. This grade-level meeting is a great time for logistics, announcements, reflections, and the introduction of new students and farewells to those who are moving away. These meetings will help students practice their listening, focus, compassion, and empathy skills.

Recently, an adult participant from a residential 8-day workshop in which we ran daily, hour-long community meetings came to me on one of the last days and said, "I didn't like the meetings at first and I sure wasn't going to speak at one. I still might not speak, but I'm glad someone will. I look forward to the meetings now." Simply giving students the opportunity to speak on a regular basis is a fundamental intention of a School of Belonging.

Intention 7: Daily Celebration and Recognition of Students

I often ask a group of teachers to reflect on a significant teacher from their school years. This exercise introduces the idea that we all can play an important role in the future lives of our students. One woman at a recent workshop spoke with a great sense of positive reflection about her fifth-grade teacher who recognized three to four students each day for something specific the teacher admired:

> *"We all knew that at some point each of us would be acknowledged, that it would happen more than once, and we all looked forward to every day of school. Today, I can look at a class picture from that year and tell you each kid's name and what his or her talents were."*

This story clearly illustrates the impact that recognition can have on students. When it becomes *ritualized*, when kids know that there is a chance that they will be seen in a positive light in front of their peers, they will anxiously look forward to every day of school. Student recognition programs should go beyond the posted honor roll lists or student-of-the-month programs and should also extend to all aspects of student life: athletics, the arts, citizenship, self-improvement, service learning, and any other gift of expression and talent demonstrated by a young person.

Some cultures use the term "parade" to signify the culminating celebration of hard work, long-term accomplishments, or the end of a natural transition. Examples would be a new marking period, the end of the school year, the end of a testing schedule, or just about anything significant that is ending, including the end of a period or era and the beginning of a new one. In *Building Classroom Communities* (2003), I presented a model for the stages of group development: Form, Norm, Storm, and Perform based on the work of Bruce Tuckman (1965). In the final stage of this model, Adjourn, the parade celebrates an appreciation of the group's hard work and focused intention. In a sense, the parade is a group recognition process that celebrates everyone within the group.

Intention 8: A Variety of Extracurricular Activities for All Students

In order to provide an inviting school climate in which all students feel involved and enthusiastic, many diverse opportunities for expression beyond academics and athletics must be provided. These opportunities can take the form of clubs, intramurals, or elective classes or offerings. Schools can survey students to determine their interests and then create extracurricular activities that would help them pursue those interests. Additionally, staff members can tap into their own interests and talents and take the initiative to offer something special for the students. The key is for schools to intentionally provide opportunities that help young people explore and discover their gifts and talents and also help them feel connected to the school community through their knowledge that the people in school do care about them.

I have often seen kids who are not involved because nothing interests them or, more to the truth, because it *feels* as if no one is interested in them. To be empathic takes the desire to know the other person, to take an interest in him or her. When opportunities for fun, expression, and connection are offered, empathy is being modeled because care for students is being practiced. As I mentioned earlier, there are many stories in which adults look back to the school experience and remember a person who was not only supportive but also helpful in unearthing an innate or invisible talent which, once identified, became that person's focal point. That innate talent often became their life's work, their life's expression, their *place of belonging. This eighth intention of a School of Belonging can bring that gift of awareness to your students.*

Intention 9: Alternative Programming

Some young people never seem to feel at home in school. They may have had an earlier school experience that was embarrassing or hurtful. Perhaps they never learned to read effectively, their math skills were low, or they never received the support they needed from home. Whatever the reason, it is crucial that a School of Belonging addresses the needs of these at-risk students as well.

Alternative programming is not a punishment or holding tank for difficult kids. No matter how it is structured—whether it provides study skills training, social skills development (including anger management), remediation in reading and math, or small groups with intensive focus from adults—an alternative program can alter the direction of a person's life. Often students who end up in alternative programs have felt disconnected from the school experience—from their peers, adults, the work, or their own academic expectations.

The primary goal of any alternative program should be to re-attach its students to the natural joys associated with discovery, learning, and positive relationships: the positive feelings that become dulled over time by negative, unsuccessful, and hurtful school events. The best way to reawaken these natural tendencies within a person is through positive, helping, and safe relationships: exactly what an alternative program can provide. Once the safety of a caring teacher-student relationship has been built, the work toward academic, social, and emotional success can begin to take shape. This is not an easy task. As an educator, you may feel like you are swimming against the tide of the ingrained, private logic of an angry, frustrated, and scared young person. During the most emotionally trying times, I seek to remember the following from Larry Brendtro and John Seita (2004), who in their fine book *Kids Who Outwit Adults,* wrote, "When working with challenging youth . . . optimism is a survival skill" (p. 152).

Intention 10: Parent Workshops

Parents must be provided with training of their own. Aside from the obvious value of offering help with one of life's most difficult challenges—raising a healthy child in challenging times—school offerings for parents will build bridges between the home and school.

The old adage "The ones who come aren't the ones who need to be here" is not always true and is a counterproductive belief. It is true that some of the people you want to attend will not, but rather than being critical, ask the question, "What is the unmet need?" This focus will help you plan strategies that encourage people to attend a parent offering.

It is important to consider the time of night for offering parent training along with childcare needs. If your high school has some sort of a peer helper program, endeavor to provide childcare at school by these students with a school advisor overseeing the situation. Additionally, more people will attend when food is provided before the event (spaghetti is always an inexpensive and tasty choice). It is important not to judge why people do not come to parent workshops. Focus instead on how to plan and implement strategies to get them there.

One way to increase interest is to offer workshops of interest to your parents. Common topics include:

- Communicating effectively with your child
- Understanding the nature of bullying and how to help your child with bullying issues
- Using effective discipline techniques
- Understanding the pressures your child faces today
- Helping your child study and do better in school

Whatever is offered, people will come if they are interested and food and childcare are provided. If you offer a monthly session, remember also to encourage attendees from the first session to bring another person to the next meeting. You will continue to draw larger and larger numbers and in the process build a sense of community among the parents and with the school, thereby creating an informal support group. This will model the school's concern for their children's well-being.

The Magic Wand

Marianne Williamson (2002) writes of intentions as magic wands: the power of thought should never be underestimated or underutilized (p. 12). There is great magic in focused thought because it begins to shape reality and take form in the lives and world around us. In schools where positive thought is the norm, you will see happier and more productive people, a greater sense of caring and generosity among staff and students, and a strong sense of belonging and connection for every one. Talking about these visions and sharing them with others is like waving the wand and saying "abracadabra." Within a short period of time, a School of Belonging will begin to be felt as it comes into form.

Essentially, the 10 intentions of a School of Belonging focus on relationships of caring that grow out of the choices of compassion, caring, generosity, and empathy. Once empathy is understood, taught, and practiced, it will make a difference for many in a school and the world. It all starts with the intention of the teacher who wants the students in his or her school to feel proud, devoted, supported, and safe. When shared, these feelings *will* make a difference in the world.

In the next and final section, I provide you with an empathy-building curriculum that uses songs from the *Teaching Empathy* CD to encourage students to have courageous conversations and learn vital social skills. This mini-curriculum incorporates many of the ideas from sections 1 and 2 in a series of lessons that have grown out of the many learning lessons I have facilitated using song, dialogue, and reflection.

Section 4

Courageous Conversations

Once you become aware of this force for unity in life, you can't ever forget it. It becomes part of everything you do . . .

—John Coltrane (1966), Jazz Musician

Teaching Empathy Through Music and Dialogue

This section provides an empathy-building curriculum which reflects many of the learning experiences I have facilitated with students in recent years. Often I would walk into a classroom with only a guitar, a song, and a process. Together, the students and I would create a collective path of social discovery—one which was true to life and therefore memorable. The lessons presented here represent the synergy of these co-creative experiences.

I call the process I use for these lessons MD (music/dialogue). This process has evolved over a number of years and has been influenced by a number of inspiring authors and educators. Before I present the lessons, I will write about those whose ideas have had the most influence on me and the MD Process. The work of these individuals and my own teaching "moments" have combined to form an approach to teaching empathy which is deeply meaningful for students and teachers. This introduction to the mini-curriculum on empathy includes guidance and suggestions on a number of key topics, including:

- Standing at the frontier
- Unearthing one's life potential
- Music/dialogue (MD)
- The tipping point
- The lessons
- The essence of empathy

Standing at the Frontier

The poet David Whyte offers a brilliant and intuitive vision of what it takes to find one's true heartfelt purpose. In order to craft one's unique path of exploration and expression in the world, he believes a person must have the opportunity, skills, and courage to stand at the frontier of one's own existence and look out onto the terrain of what is waiting to be found inside each of us. Our true potential resides in that place of mystery.

He calls the inner reflection on who we are and the courage to unearth our heartfelt identity, examine our inner longing, and understand this longing as the courageous conversation. I have used his deeply challenging call to individual exploration and expression in my workshops on social decision making through the use of music, moral dilemma dialogue, role-playing, poetry, songwriting, and reflective journaling. I have also called on the teachers and other staff members to support student efforts to apply their newfound self-awareness. The lessons and their accompanying processes in this curriculum are called courageous conversations because they have evolved from hundreds of Courageous Conversations workshops I have facilitated with students.

David Whyte's poems have had and continue to have deep meaning for me and the teachers I have shared them with. His poems have acted as "perspective markers" along our collective road of teaching expression.

Unearthing One's Life Potential

I was first introduced to Whyte's work by depth psychologist, ecotherapist, and wilderness guide Bill Plotkin, my guide during a vision quest. As part of our quest, Bill would periodically read to us a particularly relevant poem written by David.

Plotkin has developed an approach toward enhancing one's soulful way of living which he calls Soulcraft. He defines soul as "the primary organizing, sustaining, and guiding principle of a living being" (Plotkin, 2003, p. xiii): "Soulcraft is a set of experiences, ceremonies and processes that encourage a way of life that emphasizes meaning and mystery, while celebrating the depths and magnificence of our individuality" (p. 14). Since I first worked with Bill and his wilderness programs in 1998, I have sought to apply my inner discoveries to my outer expression through my teaching, writing, and music. The *Teaching Empathy* resource is an expression of what I have learned about my soul purpose in this world—that I am here to facilitate meaningful learning by creating processes and materials that help people feel a greater connection to themselves and others.

As I work with staff and students in schools, my intention is to create more caring school communities through the purposeful and compassionate choices of everyone—from the bus drivers, cafeteria monitors, and custodians to the teachers, administrators, teaching assistants, and students. When I facilitate lessons with students using music and dialogue, this is my own form of soulcraft because these practices guide the students to the frontier of their interactions with others in hopes that their caring selves will more strongly emerge. These "soulcraft lessons" have been formalized into this empathy-building curriculum.

It is important to remember that the starting point for the practice of empathy is having empathy for oneself. Students have often told me that they feel bad about things they have done in the past. My response is that each day provides them with the wonderful opportunity to gain self-awareness and move beyond the limitations of the previous day. Each day provides an opportunity for new choices with and toward others.

Plotkin talks of the importance of opening up to the two forms of nature: our inner nature and outer nature. Our inner nature is where our strong emotions and deep imagination live, though our imagination often lies dormant. We need to have empathy inward (through courageous conversations) to connect with the caring, purposeful self we are before we can travel outward with empathy for other people's inner nature and soulful ways of being. Reaching that goal would result in diversity and character education at their finest.

Music/Dialogue (MD)

These two ideas of standing at the frontier and unearthing one's life potential have been key elements in my work as a musician. Through the years, I have performed songs for students as a way to pull everyone together while we explore challenging social issues. This use of the MD Process began with a song called "Howard Gray." The lyrics of this song have consistently drawn students in on a deep emotional level, opening them up to the complexities of human feelings and dilemmas, and the power of empathic reflection and actions.

This empathy curriculum includes a recording of "Howard Gray" along with recordings of 5 other songs to accompany a sequence of 14 Courageous Conversations lessons. These lessons have evolved over time and proven to be the most contemplative for the students. The learning process for these lessons is primarily through dialogue. I define dialogue as a collective exploration of an issue with a group. I first learned about dialogue through the work of MIT professor and systems change specialist Peter Senge. In his book, *The Fifth Discipline Fieldbook* (1994), Senge presents dialogue as a group exploratory process.

Its purpose is not necessarily to come to an agreement but rather to come to an understanding of all points of view, thereby creating a common thread of connection within the group.

A class in which the practice of dialogue has become ritualized will have a higher degree of group emotional intelligence and a higher degree of empathy. The skill utilized by the teacher or group facilitator for this form of dialogue is high-level listening (p. 63). Each lesson includes scripting to facilitate open-ended dialogue. Also included are common student responses. The skill in facilitating these lessons lies in asking the appropriate follow-up questions and summaries to ensure flow, student involvement, and authentic and memorable learning.

The Tipping Point

The ultimate goal of these lessons is that somewhere within your students' experience of them, the group will reach the "tipping point" for social cultural change in the school. I first learned of the tipping point from Malcolm Gladwell (2000), who describes it as "that one dramatic moment in an epidemic when everything can change all at once" (p. 9). Change does not have to be incremental over a period of time. It can be a series of unique and rapid inter-connected events that tip things toward a different place, a new direction, or a new way of being.

I encourage you to approach these lessons with the hope that something you say, something a student says, or something that someone thinks during the lesson will have a profound impact on the future of some of the students in the room. Gladwell's concepts have given us a name for one of our ultimate goals: to facilitate a moment which could change the life of a student forever towards the positive. This notion of the tipping point is presented for grades 5–8 (and higher) in lesson 5, "Breaking the Silence: The Tipping Point" on page 167. This lesson shows students that "little things are big things": It may take one person to tip a situation or environment from emotional violence to emotional safety.

The Lessons

The 14 lessons in this mini-curriculum are divided into six lessons for grades 3–4 and eight lessons for grades 5–8 that can be adapted for grades 9–12. Some of the songs are used for both levels ("Howard Gray" and "Let Me In"), while others and their accompanying lessons are appropriate for one level only. You certainly may use the songs for either level, modifying the lessons as needed. Although the second set of lessons is recommended for grades 5–8, most of the lessons have been used successfully with high school students. For students in grades 9–12, modify the lessons as you wish to make them more accessible and relevant for this older group. Each section ends with a list of presented concepts or terms and specific follow-up extension ideas to facilitate the caring culture these lessons promote.

Each lesson is designed to be facilitated in approximately 40 minutes. I suggest you go with the energy of the group and, if necessary, facilitate some of the lessons over 2 days. A number of cross-references in the curriculum to topics covered elsewhere in *Teaching Empathy* will help you prepare to facilitate the lessons more effectively and will provide you with extension and infusion ideas. The lessons are scripted to capture the essence of the give and take dialogue that has evolved through the years as I taught these lessons. You may want to modify the way you present the information to match your own style and purpose.

The seventh song, "Mrs. Lopez, I'll Never Forget You," can be used to facilitate dialogue with your students. It has also been included for you, the educator, as a song that reflects on the emotional impact that Mrs. Lopez, my fifth-grade teacher, had on me. I hope the song will inspire you and remind you of what I wrote in section 1: *Teachers can and often do have a significant life-long impact on their students when they consciously make positive connections.*

The Essence of Empathy

One night, while driving through the back roads of New Hampshire, I listened to a tape a friend had given me only hours before. I had been contemplating a high-school leadership workshop that I would be giving in a school in which intolerance was the norm. I was searching for a way of inspiring these students to work toward change. A song came on, a ballad, and as the song's story unfolded, I found myself increasingly absorbed into its message. I pulled my car over to listen more intently. Afterward, I sat there for a long time, deeply engaged in emotional memories from my own school days as I remembered the way people were treated by peers and remembered the pain so many of us had felt. I thought of the pain so many students were still feeling in school.

That song was "Howard Gray" by Lee Domann, and that night changed my life. "Howard Gray" tells the true story of a student who is different and is ridiculed by his peers because of it. The song helps the listener identify with the realities of the way people are often mistreated.

I soon learned the song and started singing it for students, teachers, and parents in workshop settings. The universal truths communicated through Howard's story, and the emotional connections people make with the character of Howard, put listeners in touch with what I call the "essence of empathy." When you listen to Howard's story, it is difficult not to find yourself right in the middle of it, wanting to do something to change the way things are. That is the ultimate hope for the students we are working with on the issues addressed in this book. "Howard Gray" is the first song presented in section 2 (for grades 5–8) and the second song presented in section 1 (for grades 3–4). It can be used as a symbol of understanding for the entire curriculum as you use the other lessons to build on the emotional impact and sense of curiosity that it creates.

Part 1: Lessons for Grades 3–4

The six lessons that follow will introduce your students to a number of essential social skills through the use of the Music Dialogue Process (see page 117). Each lesson is presented in an easy-to-use format:

- The regular text in the lesson indicates what you can say as you teach the lesson.

- The indented text in parenthesis indicates how your students may answer a question.

- The italics text indicates what you need to do to facilitate the lesson.

Lesson 1

"Lift Me Up"

Materials: *Teaching Empathy* CD (track 6), copies of "Lift Me Up" lyrics (page 209: one per student), chart paper or flipboard, markers

This lesson teaches students about the impact of the choices they make toward others. It also introduces the use of common language to describe social choices that connect or reject. This lesson frames the sequence of lessons and songs that the students will experience in this curriculum as they explore the social skills necessary for making helpful and empathic social choices each day in school.

Part 1: What Is a Social Skill?

Today we will learn what a social skill is and how we use our social skills every day as we make choices that affect other students here at school.

Write "social skills" on the board and ask:

Who can tell me what the word "skill" means?
    (Something you do well.)

Ask a few students, one by one:

What is something you do well?

Whatever it is you do well, what does it take to become skillful at something?
    (Practice)

Yes, practice. Let's continue with the word "social." What does social mean?
> (It means talking, doing something with other people, and so on.)

Social does refer to people. When you think of skills, your social skills are the skills you need when you are with people. This lesson uses music to help us learn about a social skill.

One of the most important social skills is the skill of making a choice. What does the word "choice" mean?
> (When you pick something you want, when you make a decision.)

That's right. Some choices are easier than others. For instance, it usually is easy to choose what flavor of ice cream you want. If you always order vanilla with rainbow sprinkles on a cone, then that is an easy choice. Making a choice can be more difficult, though, when you have to choose what you will wear to school.

Have you ever had a hard time deciding what you're going to wear?
> (Yes)

Why is it so difficult to decide what you want to wear?
> (I want to look good. My mom or dad wants me to wear something different.)

That's right. Suddenly, the choice involves others and what they will think. That is what makes the choice more difficult. When choices affect others, we call them "social choices."

Draw the diagram on page 58 as you speak:

There are two kinds of social choices we make each day: connect or reject. Let's look at the connect choice first. Imagine that the little circles inside the larger circle are other students.

We call this circle the Circle of Friendship because everyone is connected. It doesn't mean that everyone inside the circle is close friends, but it does mean that they are accepted and treated kindly.

The second kind of social choice is called reject.

Draw a circle all by itself.

Connect means to be accepted as a part of the group or class. Reject can mean that the person is being teased or put down, or excluded in some way. It can also mean that the person is new, doesn't know anybody, and feels left out.

If a new kid is waiting all alone at the bus stop, is he in reject or connect?
　　(Reject)

If another boy told that kid he couldn't sit on the bus with him, what social choice would that be?
　　(Reject)

If you were sitting on the bus and saw this happen, what could you say to the rejected kid to help him feel connected?
　　(Do you want to sit with me?)

Yes! When you make a connect choice, it doesn't have to be a huge choice for you, but it can mean a lot to the other person who is receiving it—whether it's sitting together on the bus or saying hello. These are all examples of using the social skill of making a "connect" choice. Who can tell us some other examples of a connect choice you could make at school?

Part 2: "Lift Me Up"

We're now going to listen to a song called "Lift Me Up." In this song, "lift me up" means the same thing as connect and "put me down" means the same thing as reject. As you listen, read the words on the sheet I give you.

Give each student a copy of the lyrics (page 209). Then play track 6 on the Teaching Empathy CD.

After the song is completed, use the following questions to guide the student conversation:

- Has anyone ever had a bad day when nothing seemed to go right?

- What happened, and how did you feel?

- What did you need from others?

- What does the song mean when it says, "every day as you make your choices, can you hear all the voices?"

- How does it feel to be rejected? Has anyone ever felt this way?

Prepare a piece of chart paper, flipchart, or chalkboard. Record in list form the students' responses to the following questions:

- What are some specific ways that people are rejected?

- When you feel rejected, what do you need from others?

- What are some specific connect choices people can make toward one another?

We will continue to talk about the choices we make as these lessons continue. In each lesson, we will listen to a song and have a conversation about it. What is one thing you have learned in this lesson?

Lesson 2

"Howard Gray" (Part 1)

Materials: *Teaching Empathy* CD (tracks 1 and 2), copies of "Howard Gray" lyrics (page 204: one per student), chart paper or flipboard, markers

This lesson introduces students to the song "Howard Gray" as an entry to understanding the emotional impact that their social choices can have on each other.

Introduction

Today we're going to continue our lesson on social skills and social choices. Before we listen to the new song, let's review what we learned in our first lesson.

What do we mean by "social choices"?
    (Choices that involve others)

What are the two kinds of social choices?
    (Reject or connect)

Draw the reject or connect diagram on the board.

Our song today was written by a man named Lee Domann *(doe-man)*. Many years ago, Lee was a student in a tiny school in Kansas. In his school, he was in the connect circle.

Draw a new, small circle in a different color in the middle of the connect circle.

Lee was a popular kid. He had many friends. He was a good student and a good athlete.

Draw other small circles in the connect circle to represent Lee's friends.

There was another boy in Lee's class named Howard Gray. Howard was the kid nobody liked. He was on the outside wanting to be a part of the connect circle.

Draw a small circle in the reject circle to represent Howard.

Many kids in the connect circle gave Howard a hard time. They teased him and called him names. Lee felt sorry for Howard, but he chose not to leave the circle to go over and connect with Howard. Why do you think he never reached out to Howard?
(He was afraid he wouldn't get back into the circle. He didn't want to lose his popularity.)

Let's listen to the introduction to the song "Howard Gray" and then to the song itself. When the song starts, please read along with the lyrics.

Give each student a copy of the lyrics for "Howard Gray." Play tracks 1 and 2 on the Teaching Empathy *CD.*

Remember, this is a true story. Is this a story of reject or connect?
(Reject. *Some students may say "connect" because earlier in the song Lee left Howard alone.*)

Does this type of thing happen in this school? Are people ever put down?
(Yes)

This isn't a lesson about what is right or wrong. It's a lesson about what is real. Let's brainstorm answers to this question: Why are people put down? *(Write responses on a flipboard or chart paper.)*
> (Grades, they're new, skin color, clothes, they're different, they need extra help in school, people don't know them, not good at sports, people don't like them, and so on)

What is the main reason why anyone is the target of put-downs, teasing, or bullying? The answer I'm looking for is on the list if you look and think carefully.
> (Different. *Students may offer other answers, but eventually someone will say that being different is really the issue.)*

Role-play the following scenario as you share it with the class:

Let's look at why different is the reason. If I walked down a trail, came to a dark cave, and walked slowly into the cave, what would I do if I suddenly heard a roar? Would I run into the cave to see what it is?

> *(Most will call out "no!")*

Why not?
> (Because there's a bear in there or some other ferocious animal.)

Do we really know what is in there?
> (No)

What we don't know is called the unknown, and the unknown is often scary. Different and unknown can mean the same thing. When a person is different, people usually want to stay away or reject that person. Let's go back to the cave where I just heard a roar. How would I find out what is actually in the cave?

(Get a flashlight.)

A flashlight lets us see what is really in there. With people, we can really see "what is in there" by listening to them and giving them a chance. Listening to another person is the highest form of connect choice we can make because it helps us understand and see who another person really is.

We'll continue this conversation another day. For now, choose one of these three opening phrases and finish it with your thoughts:

1.   One thing I learned is . . .

2.   One thing that surprised me is . . .

3.   Right now I feel . . .

Lesson 3

"Howard Gray" (Part 2)

Materials: *Teaching Empathy* CD (track 8), unlined paper, drawing materials

This lesson continues to explore the story of Howard Gray. Students will imagine what Howard must have felt and then work together to create a visual of connecting with Howard. Students will also be introduced to role-playing as a social skills learning technique.

Instructions

Today we're going to continue talking about the story of Howard Gray and what could be done for him. Let's listen to a spoken version of the song right now.

Play track 8 of the Teaching Empathy *CD.*

Imagine for a moment what Howard must be feeling when he gets up for school each day. As you share what you think Howard felt, start your sentence with "I feel. . . ."

Allow as many students to share as possible and then ask:

If someone is afraid to come to school, how do you think they'll do in school?
    (Not so well, they'll get bad grades)

What is the reason they wouldn't do well in school?
    (They would be too afraid. You can't concentrate if you're afraid.)

Let's think about this in a different way. In a moment, you will work in pairs on an activity.

Assign partners and give each pair a sheet of paper.

Take your sheet of paper and fold it in half, corner to corner. Then open it up so you have two sides.

Now work with your partner to draw a before and after picture of Howard Gray. On the left-hand side, draw Howard before he came to our school. What was happening to him? What did he look like?

On the right-hand side, draw a picture of how Howard would look if he came to our school. What would you be doing to connect with him? Show what you would do, and be sure to show how he would feel.

After 20 minutes or so, focus the class to the front of the room with the following comments:

You may still be working on these, but I'd like to have some sharing. We will do this with a role play. A role play is sort of like acting. The best way to learn social skills is to practice them through a role play. I'd like to have some of you demonstrate your connecting strategy from your drawings by role-playing your strategy with me.

Imagine I'm Howard and I just moved here. You and your partner are trying to make a connection with me. Who would like to go first?

Role-play with at least three pairs.

I know others want to go, but we're out of time for now. If some of you wish to continue, we can do so over the next few days. But for now, what did you learn today?

If you can display the pictures to remind students of the lesson, end the lesson by saying:

When you are finished with your pictures, please hand them in to me and we'll hang them on the wall. Thank you.

Lesson 4

"Let Me In"

Materials: *Teaching Empathy* CD (track 4), copies of "Let Me In" lyrics (page 207: one per student), chart paper, markers

This lesson provides students with the opportunity to listen to the person who is being rejected. Students will learn the importance of including everyone in the connect circle. They will understand that doing so does not mean they have to like everyone, but does mean that they need to accept everyone.

Instructions

Today we're going to talk more about what it feels like to be rejected and why certain kids are rejected.

Let's review what we mean by connect choices.

Use the figure on page 58 as a model as you draw on chart paper or the chalkboard circles inside a circle and one circle all alone outside of the larger circle.

Would someone explain to us what this diagram represents?
    (The circles in a circle show connect choices. The circle all alone
    shows a reject choice.)

That's right. Today we'll listen to a new song called "Let Me In." A few years ago, another class heard the earlier lesson on making the social choice to connect or reject. At the end of the lesson, one student stood up and told the class that he was new and that no one had ever talked to him since he had moved in. He pointed at the connect diagram his teacher had put on the board and said,

"Just let me in. Give me a chance. You don't even know me." The song we'll hear today is inspired by this true story.

Is it hard to be a new student?
(Yes)

Option 1: If you have new students and think they would be willing to share, ask them the following questions:

- As you were getting ready for school, what were you thinking and what were you feeling?

- What was it like on the morning of your first day here?
    (I was nervous. I didn't know what to wear. I wondered if the kids would like me.)

Option 2: If you don't have new students or feel they would be uncomfortable with the questions, ask the class:

- How would you feel on your first morning at a new school?

- What do you think you'd be thinking and feeling as you got ready to go to school on that first day?
    (It's hard being new. It feels like you are an outsider, like you are outside of the circle.)

Give each student a copy of the lyrics for "Let Me In" as you say:

Let's listen to the song "Let Me In" and read along with the lyrics as we listen.

Play track 4 on the Teaching Empathy *CD.*

What does it mean in the song: "You don't even know what I've seen or where I've been?"
    (They don't even know the kid because he's new.)

What does it mean to be treated like the "star" while others are treated like "a fool"? Does this happen here in this school?

(Yes. Some kids are the popular kids and the others are treated poorly.)

Why is it so hard to "look inside at the person within," especially when that person is on the outside? How could looking inside help reduce the teasing and put-downs of others?

(You have to look inside. That means that inside we're all the same. My parents told me not to judge others and that would stop teasing.)

Close this lesson by having students reflect either in a journal or in pairs. Ask them to describe a time when they felt left out and were let into the circle.

Focus on what happened: What were you feeling and what did you need?

After sharing or time for journaling, close the lesson with the following question:

What will you remember about this lesson?

Optional Extension: *You may wish to offer training and practice in listening as an extension to the dialogue that takes place with this question. See the "Listening Wheel" on page 64.*

Lesson 5

"Stop and Think"

Materials: *Teaching Empathy* CD (track 7)

This lesson presents a strategy students can use when they are angry, frustrated, or confused. Students will learn how to use breathing as an effective way to re-focus their emotions in times of stress.

Instructions

Today we are going to hear a song about what to do when you get angry. Has anyone ever been angry before?

(Yes)

Is anger a bad thing?

(Yes and no)

Anger is a natural emotion. When does it become a bad thing?

(When you hurt someone else or yourself)

What kinds of things make you angry?

Dialogue with the students on this question as long as there is an interest.

What are some things you do when you are angry to calm down and feel better?

(Punch a pillow, scream into a pillow, listen to music, take a walk, cuddle with my dog, talk to an adult I trust, breathe deeply, count to 10)

We're going to listen to a song that describes a strategy we can use when we're feeling a little out of control.

Play track 7 of the Teaching Empathy *CD.*

Let's review the strategy taught in the song. What is the first step in the strategy?
(Stop)

That's right. Stop whatever you are doing. Don't say anything or do anything. Just say to yourself, "Stop."

What is the next step?
(Think)

Yes! Think about what just happened. Get it clear in your mind!

What's the third step?
(Take a breath)

Right! The third step is to take a breath. It's important that you take a **deep** breath because that will calm you down. Let me teach you how to breathe deeply to relax and focus. Watch me as I breathe in through my nose down into my chest and out through my mouth.

Breathe deeply several times as quietly as you can.

The trick is to breathe in and out as quietly as possible. Let's all give it a try. Sit up straight and breathe into your nose as quietly as you can. Keep breathing in until you can feel it way down into your chest. Now breathe out through your mouth. The louder you breathe, the less relaxed you will feel. . . . Good! Now try it again.

After the breath, you will check out what you are feeling and then decide what you will do about it. Remember, one option is to choose to do nothing about your anger, to just let it go.

Why is it important to learn how to control your anger?
(So you don't get into trouble for doing something. So you don't say something that hurts someone else's feelings.)

Here are several lines from the song:

> Stop and think.
> Take a breath.
> Check your feelings
> before you act.

These words describe a social skill called anger management. Deep breathing is helpful in other situations as well, especially if you are nervous or can't concentrate. What kind of situations might make you nervous or make it harder to concentrate?
(When you're taking a big test, during a performance at a concert, when your brother or sister takes something without asking)

So you can see, you're going to get angry or upset sometimes. If you stop and breathe before doing anything, you might make a better choice. What are you going to remember about this lesson?

Lesson 6

The Jacket

Materials: A jacket

This lesson will help students understand the importance of being patient and caring when they try to understand what another person needs. The lesson also shows how difficult teaching can be.

Instructions

Today we will have our final lesson in this program. We'll have fun while we learn an important message. Let's get started.

Imagine that I am from another planet and I have been sent to earth to learn about schools in this part of the world. I have been programmed to speak English and to know a little bit about earthlings. On my home planet, the climate is controlled: all I ever had to wear was a T-shirt, shorts, and sneakers. I never had to use a jacket although I have been taught that I should wear one on earth if it gets cold. Now it is cold out and I do not know how to put on the jacket. The challenge for you as a class is to tell me how to put on the jacket using only words. You can't use any motions.

Ask one student volunteer to come to the front of the class and tell you what to do. Follow the instructions exactly. For example, if the person says, "pick up the jacket," pick it up and drop it to the floor because you were not told to hold onto it. When you are told to "hold onto it," squeeze it with your arms.

Continue in this way for a while and then invite another volunteer to come to the front and instruct you. Be creative and have fun as you respond to the instructions, but do not allow anyone to help you put on the jacket.

Students will laugh, call out, or begin to feel frustrated.

Okay, now I'd like you to work with a partner to come up with a strategy.

Give the students a few minutes and then choose one pair as the role play continues.

Now make sure to use what you have observed from the previous students who have been up here. Okay, tell me what to do.

Within 30 seconds, allow them to help you put on the jacket. Thank the volunteers and ask them to return to their seats.

Please answer the following questions.

Here's a question for everyone who volunteered: How did you feel while trying to get me to put on the jacket?

(Have each volunteer share an answer or insight gained from the experience.)

Here's a question for the rest of the class: How did you feel when you watched the volunteers try to help me?

    (I was frustrated. It was silly. I couldn't believe you couldn't put your jacket on.)

What was . . . *[frustrating or whatever word they shared for the first question]* about this activity?

    (You didn't understand what we were telling you. You couldn't put the jacket on!)

Please know that in the first part of the activity, I wasn't going to let anyone help me put on the jacket because I wanted to show that even though putting a jacket on for you is easy, it isn't for me when I'm an alien from a planet where all I have to wear is T-shirts, shorts, and sneakers. Being told how to put on a jacket was like hearing what to do in a foreign language. I simply didn't understand!

Let's think about this problem in another way. Have any of you ever tried to teach someone younger than you how to do something?
(Yes)

Who was it? How did it go?

What did you need to do in order to be successful?
(Be patient and help without yelling.)

Thank you for taking part in this activity. What did you learn?
(It's hard to put on a jacket sometimes. People need help to do simple things. It takes a lot of patience to teach someone something.)

Let the dialogue flow in the direction that the student's answers take the group.

Remember, when you were younger you had to learn how to put on a jacket. Do you remember who taught you?
(My parents. I learned in preschool.)

Yes, someone took the time to teach you. Whether you're learning how to put on your jacket or how to do something new, it takes patience, listening, and caring to teach another person.

As we've learned in these lessons, in order to work with each other in helpful ways, we must always remember the impact of the choices we make in the moment. If we're impatient, quick to judge, or ridicule someone who is struggling, then we'll be rejecting them.

When you taught me to put on the jacket, you were really working hard to help me. Although we were having fun and I was playing a role, in real life it often takes hard work and concentration to help a person in need. This is true in our classroom, school, community, and in the world. It may not be easy to reach out and help someone else, but as we've often discussed, choosing to do that is a noble choice and always worth the effort.

What is one thing you will remember about this lesson?

Continuing the Conversation

When you have completed the section 1 sequence of courageous conversations, it is important to help students process the information presented and the lessons learned.

Here is a summary of the concepts presented:

1. Social skills

2. Social choices

3. The Circle of Friendship

4. Connect or reject

5. Different is scary

6. Stop, think, take a breath

7. Patience and understanding without judgment

The following processes and strategies will help you reinforce the lessons you have taught. You can use the content in items 1–7 above as you integrate these ideas into your classroom culture.

The Class Meeting

Hold a weekly class meeting in which you focus the dialogue on one of the concepts, particularly if the same or a related issue arises.

Morning Meeting

Establish the ritual of holding a morning meeting to build a stronger sense of connection, teach social skills, and listen to a song from the CD as a focus for the day.

Recitations

Have students volunteer to memorize the lyrics to "Howard Gray" and recite them for the class or for other classes.

The Music

Have the music from the CD playing as your students come into your classroom. Put the music in a listening center that includes activities to reinforce the messages in the songs.

Letter Writing

Have your students write letters to Howard Gray, the songwriter Lee Domann, or the author and singer David Levine. You can extend this activity by sending the letters to the publisher at:

> Publications Department
> Solution Tree
> 304 West Kirkwood Avenue
> Bloomington, IN 47404-5132

The letters will be sent to the author who will forward them on to the right people.

Common Language

Make certain words or phrases part of your classroom or school culture: "in the circle or out of the circle," "reject or connect," "Circle of Friendship," and so forth.

Concept Murals

Make a mural with the title "Lift Me Up—Don't Put Me Down." The mural could be shaped like a large hot air balloon with pictures of the "Lift Me Up" (connect) strategies placed within the balloon of the mural. Or the mural can be a long piece of butcher paper that is placed on the classroom wall or hallway.

Students can draw their connect strategies on paper cut to be small hot air balloons that are placed on the mural.

Make a friendship tree mural in the shape of a large tree. Students could add leaves for each kind or caring choice they make. Each individual leaf would list the choice, the person who made the choice, the person who benefited, and the date.

Other murals can be created to represent the concepts in the other lessons with student images, words, or both.

Poetry

Have students write poems about social choices. When students learn about different forms of poetry, they can try those forms by writing poetry on the concepts from these lessons.

Part 2: Lessons for Grades 5–8 (and Higher)

The eight lessons that follow will introduce your students to a number of essential social skills through the use of the Music Dialogue Process. Each lesson is presented in an easy-to-use format:

- The regular text in the lesson indicates what you can say as you teach the lesson.

- The indented text in parenthesis indicates how your students may answer a question.

- The italics text indicates what you need to do to facilitate the lesson.

Most of these lessons have been used successfully with high school students. Modify the lessons as you wish to make them more accessible and relevant for this older group.

Lesson 1

Through the Eyes
of Howard Gray

Materials: *Teaching Empathy* CD (tracks 1 and 2), copy of "Howard Gray" lyrics (page 204: one per student), chart paper or flipboard, markers

This lesson introduces students to the song "Howard Gray" to help them understand the emotional impact that their social choices can have on others. The concepts in this lesson also lay the foundation for the sequence of lessons and songs that students will experience in this mini-curriculum as they consider the social choices they make each day in school.

Part 1: Introducing the Lessons

Today we will begin a series of lessons which will help us understand the social culture of our school.

Write "social culture" on the board.

What does the word "culture" mean?
　　(Background, someone's religion or heritage, a way of life)

While someone's religion or heritage has cultural practices, the word "culture" actually means the way people live their lives. In our school, culture means the way we do things here. Now let's look at the word "social." What does social mean?
　　(Talking, being with people)

When we put these two words together, "social culture" means the way people are with others, how they communicate, and what they do. Each school has its own social culture with its own cultural norms.

Write the word "norms" on the board and ask:

What word is "norms" similar to?
  (Normal)

Yes, the norm is the normal way things are done. The social norms become the ways that students are expected to treat each other in school. If a norm is unchallenged or accepted, what will happen?
  (It will continue.)

If the norm is hurtful toward others and is not challenged, then it will continue as "that's just the way things are—nothing can be done about it." Have any of you ever heard of hazing? What does it mean?
  (When people have to do things they don't want to do, making kids do embarrassing things just to be on the team)

Hazing often happens in sports teams when younger players have to go through a humiliating experience of some kind to become an accepted member of the team.

If you have had an experience with hazing, you may wish to share it with the class at this point.

Hazing is an example of a social norm that is not only inappropriate and hurtful but is also potentially harmful.

Part 2: "Howard Gray"

Today we're going to look at one example of a social culture and of the social choices that were made in that culture. The song we'll hear tells the true story about something that happened in a school many years ago to the kid that no one liked—a boy named Howard Gray. The norm in that school was to give him a hard time. He was the victim of what is now known as emotional violence.

What does the word "emotion" mean?
  (A feeling)

An emotion can be a strong feeling that carries with it a lot of energy. An emotional response comes when someone is feeling strongly about "real-life" events. You might feel an emotion or two if you argue with your parents or guardian about something they want you to wear. Please raise your hand if this has happened to you. Has that happened to anyone here?
  (Many hands will go up.)

You felt strong emotions when you were arguing, didn't you? What happens in emotional violence is that one person directs strong, negative emotions toward another, and the person who receives those emotions feels as though he or she has been emotionally hurt.

This kind of violence doesn't leave the same marks as physical violence. Someone who has been hit hard in the face will get one or two black eyes. Anyone who sees the bruising can imagine the pain felt by the person who was hit. With emotional violence, the bruising and pain occurs inside.

Acts of emotional violence include name calling, teasing, put-downs, harassment, exclusion, rumors, and any other forms of non-physical aggression. Does everyone understand what I mean by emotional violence? Does it happen in our school?

(Most hands will go up.)

The song "Howard Gray" was written by one of Howard's class-mates named Lee Domann *(doe-man).* No one liked Howard. He was poor. He wasn't a good athlete or a good student. If he raised his hand to answer a question, everyone would groan. If he was assigned to work with a group, someone in the group would say, "I don't want to work with him." Do you get the picture?

The guy who wrote this song, Lee Domann, was a popular kid. He felt sorry for Howard, but he never reached out to him. Why do you think he didn't reach out to Howard?

(He didn't want to lose his friends. If he was Howard's friend, he wouldn't be cool anymore.)

Give each student a copy of the lyrics and say:

Let's listen to an introduction and the song. Please read along with the lyrics as you listen.

Play tracks 1 and 2 from the Teaching Empathy *CD. After the song is completed, someone may immediately ask, "Is that really true?" You can say that it definitely is a true story.*

Now that we've heard the song, let me ask you, "Is it real life? Does this happen in our school?"

(Yes)

Let's focus on why others are treated this way. Please answer the following questions.

Write their answers on the flipchart or board.

- Why do people put other people down?

- Why do people make emotionally violent choices toward others?

If we look at the list we just made, is there one main reason why people are put down?

(Someone will usually identify "different" or "differences" as the main reason. If not, you may bring it up.)

Why is being different the reason?

After a few answers, say:

What's different or unknown is scary. Do you remember your first day of school here? How many were nervous about the lockers, meeting new kids, the teachers, or the work?

If your students are in elementary school, you can use other examples like being the new student or going to a party and not knowing anyone.

How long did it take before you weren't nervous anymore?
     (A day, a week, I'm still getting used to it, and so on)

What changed?
     (I got to know things. It was familiar.)

The point here is that when something is unknown or different, it is scary. This is true for people, too. When a person is different or "unknown" in some way, other people will often choose to stay away from the person and reject or exclude him or her. When one person continues to be rejected as Howard Gray was, then that rejection becomes a form of emotional violence.

Why do you think the songwriter Lee Domann remembered the events of seventh grade so vividly that he was able to write the song?

(Lee always wished he had helped Howard.)

When emotional violence happens to a person or someone sees an act of emotional violence, it often becomes what is known as an emotional memory. The song "Howard Gray" is the description of an emotional memory.

We'll continue to talk about this story in the next lesson. For today, though, please answer the following question: What will you remember from this lesson?

After all who want to answer have shared, end the lesson.

Lesson 2

Dealing With Dilemmas

Materials: *Teaching Empathy* CD (track 8), chart paper or flipboard, markers

This lesson continues the exploration of the idea of emotions. Students will learn that our primary emotional need is to belong. Students will see how this need affects the choices we make and can create a dilemma situation. Students will have a second opportunity to hear the words to the song "Howard Gray."

Instructions

Today we're going to continue talking about the song "Howard Gray."

What made the biggest impression on you from our first lesson on Howard Gray?
(The song, the music, how Howard was treated)

Who can tell me what emotional violence means?
(Emotional violence is when someone's feelings are hurt, they're called names, or they're put down a lot.)

Why do people often have such a strong emotional response to Howard's story?
(It's sad. It's happened to them. It's cool [meaning "it's real"].)

We're going to listen to a spoken version of "Howard Gray." Listen carefully once again as I play it for you. If you have your copy of the lyrics from the last lesson, you can read along.

Play track 8 of the Teaching Empathy *CD.*

The story of Howard and Lee happens in schools every day. Do you agree that this kind of thing happens in this school? What we are learning about is "real life." Let me explain what I mean by real life by asking the following questions. If any of the things I ask are true or "real" for you, raise your hand.

Have you ever changed your clothes at least once before leaving for school?

Why are people so concerned about the clothes they wear?
(They want to be in style. They don't want to be laughed at. They want to fit in.)

Have you ever been in a class when you thought you knew the answer to a question but were unsure so you didn't raise your hand? Then someone raised a hand, gave the same answer, and it was the right one. Have you done this?

Why didn't you raise your hand?
(I didn't want to get the answer wrong. I didn't want to be laughed at.)

Here's one more question. It's a little different but be honest when you answer. Raise your hand if this one is real life for you. Have you ever been with your friends when they started talking about a movie they'd seen but you hadn't? Did you act as if you'd seen the movie?

Why would someone do this?
(To be cool, to fit in, to not feel left out)

Let me show you a diagram of what this looks like and how it affects the social choices we make every day.

Draw the diagram on page 58 on chart paper or a chalkboard as you continue:

Imagine the little circles inside the larger circle are other students. We call this larger circle "connect." To be inside the circle is to be connected, to belong, and to be cool. It doesn't necessarily mean that every one is good friends, but it does mean that everyone is accepted. It is emotionally safe.

The other circle is alone, outside, and disconnected. We call this circle "reject."

Each of these diagrams represents a social choice: connect or reject. To choose connect is to connect with others and to accept them. To choose reject is to exclude or intentionally hurt another person or to feel different and alone, outside of the group.

In the song "Howard Gray," Lee Domann wanted to leave the connect circle but he was afraid that he wouldn't be let back in. Have you ever made a choice to do something you knew you shouldn't do but you did it anyway?

    (Yes)

Have you ever gotten in trouble for a choice you made?

    (Yes)

If you've ever gotten in trouble for a choice you made, when an adult asked, "What were you thinking?" did you say, "I don't know"?

At this point, the class will be highly engaged and the opportunity for a memorable experience will be high.

It is not that you "didn't know": you were confused or unsure. In other words, you were in the middle of a dilemma. Who knows what the word "dilemma" means?

(A problem)

A dilemma is a problem because it means having to make a social choice, and there is more than one choice which makes sense or has merit.

Has anyone ever seen a cartoon of a person who has the devil on one shoulder and an angel on the other? *(See section 2, page 59.)* A dilemma is like that. Although we don't have an angel and a devil on our shoulders, we do have two conflicting (opposing) thoughts in our mind. One voice whispers, "Do the right thing," while the other voice yells out, "Do what you need to do to be cool, to be accepted." It is hard not to listen to the one that is yelling at us.

Here are a few moral dilemmas:

1. Your best friend hassles another kid and you think it's wrong. Your moral dilemma is in choosing whether to ask your friend to stop or to say nothing and allow the hassling to continue.

2. Your friend forgot to bring homework home last night and pleads with you to copy your homework. Your moral dilemma is in choosing whether or not to give your homework to your friend.

In the song "Howard Gray," the storyteller has the dilemma of whether or not he should leave the connect circle and be Howard's friend or go along with the others in an effort to be accepted by the group (staying in the circle). What are some of the moral dilemmas you face in school each day?

After some dialogue, close by saying:

When you don't know what to do, ask yourself this question: If I make this choice, am I choosing to reject another person (emotional violence) or accept that person for who they are?

Let's think about what we just shared with each other. This hasn't been a lesson on what you should or shouldn't do or how you should think. Instead, this lesson reminds us that we all need to think about the choices we make each day and how these choices affect others, including ourselves.

Lesson 3

The Courage of the Heart (Part 1)

Materials: *Teaching Empathy* CD (track 4), copy of "Courage" lyrics (page 206: one per student), chart paper or flipboard, markers

This lesson presents an alternative definition of courage to mean "with heart or passion." This notion of courage is applied to acting empathically which means to follow one's core beliefs—possibly going against one's peers.

This lesson includes a reference to how Martin Luther King, Jr., followed his heart and acted with courage. You can enhance this part of the lesson by preparing to play for your students an excerpt from one of his famous speeches. His speech entitled "I Have a Dream" is available in print and audio at www.americanrhetoric.com/speeches/Ihaveadream.htm.

Instructions

In today's lesson, we'll hear a new song that could be the female version of the song "Howard Gray." The song tells the story of a girl named Diane who is the new kid in school that no one likes. The person telling the story (the songwriter) has a similar moral dilemma as the writer of the song "Howard Gray": whether to reach out to Diane or not.

Who can tell me what dilemma means? We talked about this last time.

> (It's when you have a problem, when you have to make a difficult decision)

After a brief review, continue:

Even though a person often knows in his or her heart what the "right social choice" is when interacting with others, it can be a challenge to follow one's heart. Let's look at some examples of real-life dilemmas which show how hard it can be to make the "right choice."

What would you do if you found $20 on the bus? What is the moral dilemma, what would you do, and what is your reasoning?

What would you do if your friend asked you not to go to a party because she wasn't invited? You like the person who is having the party and really want to go to it. What is the moral dilemma, what would you do, and what is your reasoning?

After discussion, say:

Today's song is about the challenge of following one's heart and about how difficult and intense some moral dilemmas can be. Before I play it, there are three historical references in the song that you'll need to understand. The lyrics include the phrase "Gas chambers, bombers, and guns in Auschwitz, Japan, and My Lai." These words are used to remind us of three different events in history.

Gas chambers in Auschwitz refers to what?
(The Holocaust when the Jews were sent to concentration camps. Auschwitz was one of those camps. It was referred to as a death camp because the people who were sent to it either died or wished they had. People were tortured and killed there.)

Facilitate some discussion on this situation, being sensitive to the age, experience, and make-up of the group.

Does anyone know what "bombers in Japan" refers to?
>(Some may say Pearl Harbor although eventually someone will say the atomic bombs or "nuclear bombs.")

This phrase is about the atomic bombs that were dropped on Hiroshima and Nagaski to end World War II in that part of the world. It was a horrible time, and thousands died or became ill because of the radiation.

The last reference in the song is to guns in My Lai. Does anyone know what that refers to?
>(An incident in the Vietnam War: most students will not know this reference)

This refers to a terrible incident which took place during the Vietnam War in a village known as My Lai. An American platoon was ordered to go into the village on a "search and destroy mission." When they were done, they had killed approximately 300 women, children, and elderly people. Their commander William Calley was convicted of the premeditated murder of 22 villagers and given a dishonorable discharge. That means he was forced out of the army.

We will hear these three references as we listen to the song. Please read along with the lyrics as we listen.

Give each student a copy of the lyrics. Play track 3 from the Teaching Empathy CD.

After the song is ended, say:

The name of the song is "Courage." Why is it called "Courage"?
(Because the singer invited Diane to the party)

What does the word "courage" mean?
(To be brave, to do something even when you are afraid)

Courage comes from the old French word "cuer" which means heart or with heart. Courage in this context means to follow one's heart or passionate beliefs when making a difficult decision, when in the middle of a moral or social dilemma. Following one's heart is often a courageous act because a person may risk his or her social standing or place in the circle of acceptance. Who in recent history has followed his or her heart and acted with courage?
(Martin Luther King, Jr.)

When his name is mentioned, ask:

Could someone describe how Dr. King spoke when he was giving a speech—not **what** he said, but **how** he said it.
(Strong, confident, like he was singing, like he believed in what he was saying)

He was in his cuer: he spoke from his heart and stood strongly by what he felt was the right thing.

(At this point, you may wish to play a recording of Martin Luther King giving a speech.)

Did he do all of the work of the civil rights movement?
(No)

What he did do was to lead and inspire others toward change with his words, his actions, and his heart—his cuer. Let me draw a diagram of what it means to be in your heart.

Draw the following diagram on chart paper or the chalkboard.

When we make decisions, they either come from our head or our heart. Your heart is where your courage resides. It is where you know what the right thing to do is. Your head is where you think about what you need to do to gain acceptance. It is said that "the longest journey to take is from the head to the heart." What does this phrase mean to you?

(It's hard sometimes to do what you know is right if it means going against your friends.)

After dialogue, close by asking:

What will you remember from this lesson?

This lesson could be extended as a journaling session. Topics could include:

- *What is your passion (cuer)?*

- *When have you made a decision based on what you thought your friends were doing?*

- *Write about a time you went against the crowd and made a choice that turned out well.*

- *Why is Martin Luther King considered an American and world hero?*

Lesson 4

The Courage of the Heart (Part 2)

Materials: *Teaching Empathy* CD (track 9), chart paper or flipboard, markers

This lesson continues to focus on the inherent challenges of social decision making. It reinforces the importance of following one's heart even when the head or thoughts are in another direction.

A section of this lesson presents an excellent opportunity to use the fishbowl strategy described on pages 84–89. As you review the lesson below, also review the fishbowl strategy and decide whether you will use it as well.

Instructions

Today we are going to continue exploring the idea of courage. What does courage mean?
    (To follow your heart)

Draw the head-heart diagram on page 161.

Look at this diagram. Where does courage reside?
    (In the heart)

I'm going to read some of the lyrics from the song "Howard Gray." As I do so, notice where I point:

    Deep down (point to the heart)
    I kind of liked you
    but I was too afraid *(point back up to the head)*

to be a friend to you,
Howard Gray.

You can see how it works. We are constantly bouncing back and forth between what we think we should do and what we know or feel we should do.

Let's continue with these lyrics from "Courage":

Diane is a girl that I know.
She's strange like she doesn't belong.
I don't mean to say that that's wrong, *(point to the heart)*
we don't like to be with her though. *(point to the head)*

"I acted like nothing was wrong." Is that head or heart?
(Head)

"When I saw Diane start to cry." Head or heart?
(Heart)

Let's listen to the spoken version of the song "Courage."

Play track 9 from the Teaching Empathy *CD.*

Have any of you ever gone along with the crowd even though you knew what you were doing probably wasn't the right thing to do?
(Yes)

What was the reason?
(I didn't want to be rejected. I didn't want to lose my friends. I was afraid what other kids would think about me.)

After a brief dialogue, continue with the following statement or invite students to read from the lyrics instead of you:

I'm going to read the following set of lyrics aloud to you from "Courage."

> *In one class at Taft Junior High,*
> *we study what people have done*
> *with gas chamber, bomber, and gun*
> *in Auschwitz, Japan, and My Lai.*
>
> *I don't understand all I learn.*
> *Sometimes I just sit there and cry.*
> *The whole world stood idly by*
> *to watch as the innocent burned.*
>
> *Like robots obeying some rules,*
> *atrocities done by the mob,*
> *all innocent just doing their job,*
> *and what was it for—was it cool?*
>
> *The world was aware of these crimes*
> *but nobody cried out in shame.*
> *No heroes, and no one to blame?*
> *A story that no one dared tell.*

What doesn't the storyteller understand?
> (How people could do this)

When she doesn't understand, she is in her head *(point to the head)* because she can't find any reason why people would do this to others.

When she "just sits there and cries," she is in her heart. *(Point to the heart.)* She is in her emotions.

Dilemmas take us from our head to the heart. The heart is where courageous actions come from.

The following question could be presented and explored using the fishbowl strategy on pages 84–89. However you present this material, remember that it is a sensitive issue and that both positions must be stressed. One position might be if more people spoke out, that action may have stopped the violence and saved people's lives. Another position might be if someone spoke out, that person and/or his or her family may have lost their lives. It was not an easy choice, and there really is no right answer.

Here's a moral reasoning question for you to consider. This reflects the intense moral dilemma that many German citizens faced during the Holocaust which occurred during World War II. German citizens had friends, neighbors, and co-workers who were the victims of the crimes committed by the German government. If these civilians did not speak out against the acts that led to these "atrocities," were they as much to blame as those who were committing the acts?

After some significant dialogue, write the words "social norms" on the board and ask:

If someone in our school is the victim of emotional violence and another student, a bystander, doesn't do something to stop it, is that person as much to blame as the person or people who are making the hurtful choices?
  (Yes, because if they don't say anything, it will continue and may get worse.)

After dialogue, say:

Reflect on what we've shared today and complete one of the following thoughts:

One thing I learned is . . .

One thing I keep thinking about is . . .

One thing I will do differently is . . .

I wonder . . .

Lesson 5

Breaking the Silence: The Tipping Point

Materials: Chart paper or flipboard, markers

This lesson identifies how challenging it can be to stand up for what one believes is the right thing. Students will understand how important it is to identify their beliefs regarding how people should be treated (guiding principles or power code) and to know that one prosocial choice on their part could be the tipping point away from emotional violence and toward emotional safety.

Instructions

Let's start today's lesson by reviewing what the word "emotion" means. Who can tell me?

(Strong feelings)

It's important to understand what emotions are because we must know the difference between emotional violence and physical violence when we look at the social culture of our school. What is the difference between the two?

(Emotional violence hurts your feelings and physical violence hurts your body.)

We can also look at the differences between a physical need and an emotional need. What are some physical needs all people have?

(Water, food, clothing, shelter)

If someone says "love," point out that love is an emotional need and you can move into the next question.

What are some emotional needs?
(Belonging, love, friends, healthy relationships, independence, a sense of control or power)

Remember, emotional needs live in the heart and not in the head. The desire to have these needs met is what affects our choices, like doing something you know you shouldn't do but you do it anyway to gain acceptance.

We've already established in previous lessons that some forms of emotional violence exist in our school. How many of you feel the teachers do not know how much emotional violence actually happens?
(Most hands will go up.)

Where does it usually happen?
(Cafeteria, at recess, bus, hallways, outside the school)

What can you tell us about those places?
(Not a lot of teachers are around)

As you can see, emotional violence is often undetected because it usually happens where there is minimal or no adult supervision. With no adults nearby, the student bystanders play an important role in the social culture of a school. They help determine if the school is emotionally safe or filled with emotional violence.

Raise your hand if you have ever known that someone was being harassed or hassled and you didn't do anything to stop it?

Why does this happen?
(You don't want them to do it to you. You don't want to go against your friends. You weren't friends with the kid who was being bullied.)

Here's something to think about. The University of Colorado Conflict Research Consortium (www.conflict.colorado.edu/) found that 10% of students are bullies, 15% of students are victims, and 75% of students are bystanders.

Draw a large circle on flipchart paper or the chalkboard. As you say the following, draw 10 smaller circles in the large circle:

If I put 10 circles inside this larger circle and these 10 circles represent students in a school, how many of these circles are bullies if 10% of students are bullies?

  (One)

If 15% are the victims, approximately how many circles would that be?
  (Two)

How many circles are left?
  (Seven)

Your figure may look like the one below. Use the letter B to identify the bully and the letter V to identify the victims.

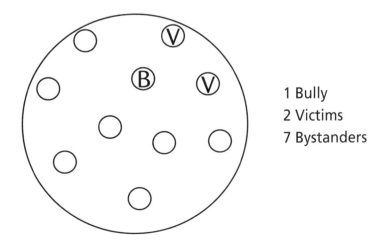

1 Bully
2 Victims
7 Bystanders

These seven circles represent the bystanders: they know what is happening and they feel it is wrong, but they do not have the "cuer" to stop it in some way. How many bystanders do you think it would take to tip the scale from emotional violence to emotional safety?

You may get a variety of answers, but the one to look for is "one." Once someone answers "one," say:

That's right! Let me stress that all seven bystanders do not feel that emotional violence is right. When one person has the courage to stand up for what is right—and in this situation it is the right everyone has to feel emotionally safe—then the other bystanders will follow the lead and also speak up. When this happens, the emotional violence will often end or be significantly reduced. A new cultural norm will have been established—one that says that "putting others down is not a cool thing to do in this school." When one or two people make a difference for many—in this case, speaking up for someone's rights and shifting the social culture—we call this the tipping point because their actions "tip" a situation from emotional violence to emotional safety.

How do you go from being a bystander to being someone who stands up for what you believe? There are ways to stand up for your beliefs or another person's right to feel safe in school. Some are considered high risk, while others are low risk.

Some high-risk intervention choices are reaching out to the victim, asking the bully why he or she is acting this way, or just telling that person to stop.

Why are these considered high-risk intervention choices?
   (Because you put yourself at risk in some way)

Here are some low-risk intervention choices:

- Tell an adult in the school who you trust what is happening. Since you were very young, you've probably been told, "Don't be a tattle tale." But it's important to separate these words, "tattle" and "tale." Tattling usually means that you're trying to get another person in trouble. Telling is not **tattling** to get someone in trouble but a principled action of **telling** to get help for another person.

- In school one low-risk choice can be provided by installing a bully box outside of the guidance office. People can put anonymous tips in the box when they want to get help for someone else.

What are some other tipping point strategies we could implement here, moving things toward emotional safety?

(Encourage the person who is being bullied. Sit with him or her in the cafeteria or on the bus. Ask the bully to stop acting that way.)

We've covered a lot today. Thanks to everyone. Let's close by completing one of the following phrases with your thoughts from today:

- One thing that surprised me is . . .
- One thing I will do differently is . . .
- Right now I feel . . .

Lesson 6

"Let Me In"

Materials: *Teaching Empathy* CD (track 4), a copy of the "Let Me In" lyrics (page 207: one copy for each student)

This lesson presents an alternative perspective as students listen to the voice of the person who is being victimized. Students will be challenged to look at others for who they are, not for what they seem to be.

Instructions

Today we're going to look at the issue of emotional violence from another perspective: through the eyes of the victim. What does the word "perspective" mean?

    (A point of view)

Let's review the connect-reject diagram.

Draw the figure from page 58 on the flipchart or the chalkboard.

Would someone explain to us what this diagram represents?
    (The big circle means that the kids inside of it are connected, and the little circle means that the kid is rejected.)

Today we will listen to a new song called "Let Me In." When we listen, we'll hear the point of view of the person who is outside the circle.

Give each student a copy of the lyrics and say:

Please read along with the lyrics as you listen.

After you play track 4 from the Teaching Empathy *CD, say:*

What does the following phrase mean in the song: "You don't even know what I've seen or where I've been?"

> (You shouldn't judge another person without even knowing him or her. It's like when someone says, "Don't judge a book by its cover.")

After brief dialogue, say:

What does it mean to be treated like the "star" while others are treated like "a fool"? Does this happen here in this school? Raise your hand if this happens here.

Why is it so hard to "look inside at the person within," especially when that person is on the outside?

> (If you don't ever hang out with someone or you don't know them, it's hard to understand them.)

How could looking inside help reduce the teasing and put-downs of others? What skill is necessary in order to work toward understanding someone better?

> (If you work hard to get to know someone, you probably wouldn't put them down. You might even like them. Listening helps me understand someone else better.)

You may wish to offer listening training and practice with the Listening Wheel on page 64 as an extension to the responses to this question.

This lesson can be closed in one of three ways:

1. Have the students write a journal entry that focuses on a time when they were "let in" when they were feeling "left out."

2. Have the students share with the class a time they were feeling left out when someone "let them in."

3. Have students reflect either in a journal in pairs or with the class on the following questions: Share a time when you were let in when you were feeling left out. What did you feel? What did you need?

After students share or write in their journals, end the lesson by asking:

What will you remember about this lesson?

Lesson 7

"We All Have a Gift"
(The Circle of Courage Song)
(Part 1)

Materials: Teaching Empathy CD (track 5), copy of "We All Have a Gift" lyrics (page 208: one per student), chart paper or flipboard, markers

The Circle of Courage represents a developmental framework that utilizes the Native American medicine wheel (see page 40 for more information). When students hear the song "We All Have a Gift," they will understand that each direction on the medicine wheel has a learning preference that is associated with a totem animal.* Students will see that each person has his or her own unique gift. When these are honorably combined with the gifts of others in the group, the entire group can create a synergy of collective community achievement. (See www.crystalinks.com/bighorn.html for more information on the origin of the medicine wheel.)

Instructions

Today we'll continue our lessons on social choices by learning about one way the Native Americans explain the choices people make. These people believe that each person's personality (a

---

*The qualities and accompanying totem animals for the Circle of Courage were conceptualized by Frank Mulhern, Poughkeepsie City Schools, and John Mancusco, Pius Youth and Family Services, Bronx, New York, and are used by permission. For information on Circle of Courage training for schools using the totem framework, contact Frank Mulhern of The Circle of Courage Learning Community, 160 Union Street, Poughkeepsie, NY 12601, or e-mail fmulhern@pcsd.k12.ny.us.

person's gifts and preferences) is represented by the qualities of a specific animal.

Someone who is a fox, for example, is able to watch and know what is going on with others without being noticed; some would say it is almost as if the person were camouflaged. This keen observation serves a fox well for he or she is able to anticipate things before they happen and in the process protect him- or herself and others.

Native Americans also look to the four directions on what they call the medicine wheel for guidance and understanding. They think of "medicine" as healing, and they believe that the most complete healing or "coming together" happens as a circular process. That's why their medicine wheel is circular. Let's look at the four directions of this circle.

The Native Americans believe that at different times in a person's life, he or she will be on a different direction inside the circle. We start with the east. This direction represents new beginnings. The sun rises in the east at the beginning of each new day. The person of this direction is a visionary who is always looking for new ways of doing things. He or she likes to invent or visualize things.

We then move to the south. This direction represents a clarity of diverse viewpoints. The person of this direction is able to see the whole picture. Think of the southern sun in the noon sky when it is at its brightest. The person of this direction is the peacemaker who wants all people to get along and work things out.

The next direction we consider is the west. This direction represents mystery and the desire to reflect on the meaning of the day's events. The sun sets in the west, bringing with it the coming darkness of night. The person of the west is the keeper of tradition, someone who puts everything in its place and tries to keep things in perspective as a way of grounding him- or herself to the present set of circumstances. This person likes to organize people and situations as a way of creating concrete meaning and understanding.

The final direction of the medicine wheel is the north. This direction represents wisdom from experience and the solitary opportunity to practice the "discipline of presence" as one looks ahead to the next day's dawn. This person is the tireless worker who gets things done before going to sleep. He or she is task oriented and likes to complete tasks before moving on to new endeavors.

Now that we have quickly learned about the characteristics of each direction, please select the direction on the wheel that best matches how you see yourself. While there may be a little of each direction in all of us, there is usually one dominant direction which stands out.

When all of the students have selected one, present the final symbol of the wheel, the totem animal.

Not only does each direction on the medicine wheel have its own set of characteristics, each one also has what is known as a totem animal.

The east's totem is the eagle, the bird's eye view. This animal is able to see the big picture. Sometimes people of this direction will have great ideas but might not always follow through on them.

The south's totem animal is the deer, the peacemaker for all. Sometimes a person of this direction wants to talk everything out before moving on.

The west's totem animal is the bear. This is the person who stands up strongly for what he or she believes in. Sometimes a person of this direction is rigid in his or her beliefs and may be reluctant to consider alternative ideas.

The north's totem animal is the buffalo. This person will finish the project or task no matter what. Sometimes a person of this direction will knock people over on his or her way to accomplishing the task.

Now that you have learned about the medicine wheel, your dominant direction, and your totem animal, read along with the lyrics as we listen to the song "We All Have a Gift."

Give each student a copy of the lyrics and play track 5 from the Teaching Empathy *CD.*

We'll continue learning about the medicine wheel next time. For now, please complete one of the following phrases:

1. One thing I learned . . .
2. One thing that surprised me . . .
3. Right now I feel . . .

Lesson 8

"We All Have a Gift" (Part 2)

Materials: Chart paper or flipboard, copy of the medicine wheel (page 181), markers

In this lesson, students continue to explore the idea that people have different styles or preferences when working with others. Students will participate in a class meeting and a fishbowl activity. See pages 80 and 84 for specific directions for these two activities.

Instructions

In our last lesson, we learned about the four directions of the Native American medicine wheel. Do you remember your dominant style and direction?

Show a visual of the medicine wheel with the directions, descriptions of each direction, and the totem animals (see page 181).

Divide the class into four distinct groups: Easterners, Southerners, Westerners, and Northerners. Have them sit together in four different areas in the room. Give each group a piece of chart paper and markers.

Use a marker to draw a line that divides your chart paper in half. Work as a group to brainstorm on the top half of your piece of chart paper what you like about your individual tendencies. Then brainstorm on the bottom half of the chart paper how your preferences may get in the way when you work with people who come from other directions on the wheel. For example, Westerners can sometimes become very controlling and may have a hard time working with Easterners who aren't always as concrete in their thinking as the people from the West.

After the groups have had ample time to talk about the questions, continue:

Now that you have examined the strengths and challenges of your direction, I want each group to select two representatives to come into the center of the room. Then we'll all experience what is known as a fishbowl.

Have the class sit in chairs that form a circle around the representatives from each group. Students in the circle observe what the representatives in the middle—the fish in the fishbowl—do and say.

Fishbowl Questions

Round 1: What did your group say they liked about their direction?

Round 2: What were some of the challenges or conflicts your direction faces when working with others?

After two rounds, open the group up to a focused class meeting and help students process what they have learned with the following questions:

- What have you learned about people with other styles?

- How can this information help you when are in conflict working with or spending time with someone from another direction?

- What is something that surprised you about this lesson?

Medicine Wheel

East (Eagle)

Visionary

- Looks for new ways to do things
- Likes to invent or visualize things
- May not always follow through on ideas

West (Bear)

Meaning

- Puts everything in its place
- Organizes people and situations to create meaning
- May be rigid in beliefs

South (Deer)

Peacemaker

- Sees the "big picture" in a situation
- Wants everyone to get along and work things out
- May want to talk everything out before moving on

North (Buffalo)

Wisdom

- Finishes the project no matter what
- May "knock people over" on the way to finishing tasks

Continuing the Conversation

Once you have completed this sequence of eight Courageous Conversations, or lessons, it is important to process the information which was presented and the lessons which were learned.

Here is a summary of the concepts presented:

1. Social culture
2. Cultural norms
3. Emotional violence
4. Emotional safety
5. Moral dilemmas
6. Reject/connect
7. Courage (*cuer*)
8. Head/heart
9. Emotional needs
10. Bystanders
11. High-risk interventions
12. Low-risk interventions
13. Tattling/telling
14. Perspective
15. The Medicine Wheel/Circle of Courage and its directions

The following activities will help you extend and reinforce the concepts presented in the lessons.

The Class Meeting

Hold a series of weekly class meetings in which you focus the dialogue on one of the concepts in these lessons, particularly if a related issue comes up.

Planning

Have students use the SNAP planning model in the appendix on page 198 to plan specific bully-free programs and related activities.

Moral Dilemmas

Periodically hold a moral dilemma session with your students. Moral dilemma dialogue sessions offer situational practice for empathy and its companion social skills, keeping the students focused on the daily challenges inherent in their social lives. See the section on symbolic teaching on page 30 for more information.

Recitations

Have students volunteer to learn the recitations of the lyrics of either "Howard Gray" or "Courage" to perform for your class, for other classes, or for younger classes as part of a lesson on caring choices. It is very powerful when a high school or middle school student presents a lesson on "Howard Gray" for an elementary class.

The Music

Play the music from the *Teaching Empathy* CD for your students from time to time, and encourage them to write their own songs or poems about "real-life" social issues.

Letter Writing

Have your students write letters to Howard Gray, the song-writer Lee Domann, or the author and singer David Levine. You can extend this activity by sending the letters to the publisher at:

> Publications Department
> Solution Tree
> 304 West Kirkwood Avenue
> Bloomington, IN 47404-5132

The letters will be sent to the author who will forward them on to the right people.

Common Language

Make the following words or phrases a part of your classroom or school culture: "in the circle or out of the circle," "the tipping point," "reject or connect," "head or heart," "cuer," "perspective," and "dilemma."

The Four Directions

Continue to refer to the various directions of the medicine wheel as a way to gently remind everyone that we all are different and have different styles and gifts.

Part 3: They're Playing Our Song(s)

There are two ways to imagine what might happen with the work we do with young people: it will make a difference or it won't. In *The Tipping Point: How Little Things Can Make a Big Difference* (2000), Malcolm Gladwell writes of the stickiness factor as that which makes something memorable (p. 91). I believe the stickiness factor is emotional: feeling emotions can be learning. If you have a deep feeling associated with an event, you will not forget that event or how you felt. In the book *Lost Boys: Why Our Sons Turn Violent and How We Can Save Them* (1999), James Garbarino writes that "as children pass into adolescence they are particularly vulnerable to melodrama and sentimentality" (p. 140). This explains on some level why many young people respond so deeply to "Howard Gray" and the other songs I present in these and other social skills lessons. The music facilitates an emotional and sometimes sentimental experience that they will not forget.

I have always known on an intuitive level that songs can have a powerful effect on learning and memory. I call this truth the "they're playing our song" phenomenon. One common way this phenomenon occurs is when a person hears a song from his or her past and immediately enters into the sentimental and emotional memories from that time. Any strong emotional experience becomes an imprinted moment, especially for a young person. This imprinting forever places the experience somewhere in the psyche of that child. I also see this phenomenon happen when I return to a school and have students come up to me to tell me they remember the songs we did and messages involved and then say they want to hear the songs again.

Music can be used as the vehicle to create an emotionally coded learning event. If a song is relevant to the students' daily lives, that song and the group dialogue to reinforce its message are likely to positively shape a student's attitude and accompanying behavior. The concepts that are discussed are not necessarily new to the students. The idea that one should treat others fairly and not reject them will not be a new idea for many students. What is different, though, is the approach of combining powerful songs with group dialogue. That approach can make all the difference in terms of creating a deeply imprinted memory.

My Personal Tipping Point

Who could have predicted that on a chilly October night, a 20-minute ride home with a cassette playing in my car would become the tipping point for me in unearthing my life's work? The 4 minutes I spent listening to "Howard Gray" for the first time and the emotional memories it triggered in me began a deeply personal journey which I am continuing today. There will always be young people who need a touchstone on which to ground themselves emotionally. Their own personal tipping points could come from the music and the courageous conversation they experience during one of the lessons in this mini-curriculum. Once reached, this tipping point can lead them toward greater depth of meaning in their lives and provide renewed optimism and hope as they seek to find what the poet David Whyte (2001) would call the occupation of a call of creation, living in an "enormously present" way in the lives which have been reserved just for them.

Books

The following books and their authors inspired the creation of these Courageous Conversations and may inspire you as you introduce the concepts in the book into your classroom and school:

- *Crossing the Unknown Sea: Work as a Pilgrimage of Identity* by David Whyte (2001)

- *The Fifth Discipline Fieldbook: Strategies and Tools for Building a Learning Organization* by Peter Senge and others (1994)

- *Soulcraft: Crossing Into the Mysteries of Nature and Psyche* by Bill Plotkin (2003)

- *The Tipping Point: How Little Things Can Make a Big Difference* by Malcolm Gladwell (2000)

Afterword

The Empathic Journey

In the introduction to this book, I wrote that young people have a great deal of energy which manifests itself in the form of strong emotions: emotions that we can help them harness in positive ways as they move along their life path of social decision making. Emotion is what fuels our social choices and empathy can be seen as the high-octane emotional fuel. Empathy in practice puts forth what Daniel Goleman and his colleagues refer to as "a resonance—a reservoir of positivity that frees the best in people" (Goleman, Boyatzis, and McKee, 2002, p. ix).

When a school is emotionally safe, and when the staff and students receive training and workshop experiences relevant to their own social and emotional learning needs, resonance will be a cultural norm and will generate the inspiration, creativity, and discovery necessary for forward thinking that is positive, caring, and hopeful. My hope is that what I have written and recorded (the music) for this resource will *resonate* with you, inspiring you to make a difference in the lives of the young people with whom you work every day.

The Chain of Responsiveness

As I was preparing the manuscript of this book in its final stages for readers, I had the urge late one Friday night to e-mail Daniel Goleman to invite him to read the book before it was published. Dr. Goleman has written two best-selling books on emotional intelligence and co-wrote *Primal Leadership: Learning to Lead with Emotional Intelligence* (Goleman, Boyatzis, McKee, 2004). His work has influenced me greatly, and I thought it would be exciting to get his feedback on this resource. By 7:30 the next morning, he had e-mailed me back that he was interested and would read the manuscript if his busy schedule allowed. I was thrilled and encouraged by his modeling of what he teaches: that personal contact and responsiveness can make a major difference in people's lives. The events over the next 3 days proved this to be true.

After reading Dr. Goleman's e-mail, I pulled two of his books *(Emotional Intelligence* and *Working with Emotional Intelligence)* off of my shelves to re-read sections of them. This quick self-study was a reminder of just how important social nuances are when it comes to feeling connected and happy. Throughout the next 2 days, I found myself reaching out just a little more than I usually do in all social situations: things like a smile to a passing person, holding a door open, and expressing appreciation to those close to me.

The following Monday, I was preparing to teach five periods of social skills lessons to seventh graders in a local middle school. It was the final lesson of the year for me with them and I had been searching for a creative and inspiring closure experience. Suddenly I realized I could teach them about emotional intelligence. I wrote a lesson comparing IQ to EI in which students were asked to define what success meant to them and what it took to be successful. We then spoke of EI and I helped them understand that the social skills we had been learning—listening, empathy, anger management, stress management, supporting others, and asking for help—were all emotional skills. That lesson was one of the most successful, energetic, and enlivening sessions of my entire time with this group, and I had been working with them since fifth grade. One boy told us that success meant three things to him: "I pass school, I get a job as an auto mechanic, and I have a happy home." At the end of the lesson, as the students were leaving the room, one girl with a huge grin stopped and said, "Thanks, David. I learned a lot."

When I wrote of the 10 intentions of the School of Belonging, I said that an intention is like a magic wand which, once picked up, can make significant positive change. I am sure that Dr. Goleman receives hundreds of e-mails, and it must be challenging to respond to inquiries like mine in such a timely manner. The fact that he did demonstrates the intention of responsiveness and honor. The events which his e-mail led to in my life made a big difference in many people's lives in the smallest of ways but perhaps also in significant ways as well.

A Call to Action

I encourage you to act on what you have learned in *Teaching Empathy* as soon as you can after completing this book. You may want to focus on the strategies in the first two sections or you may feel a need to begin teaching the lessons from the mini-curriculum in section 4. Or you may wish to use the following framework to guide your efforts:

Listen to track 2, "Howard Gray," on the *Teaching Empathy* CD.

Reflect on the feelings you experience when you listen to the song.

Ask yourself, What emotional memories does this song bring back to me?

Think of one student you are reminded of when you hear this song.

What are you going to do to meet this child's emotional needs?

Over the next 5 days in school, intentionally use specific caring strategies to meet this child's needs. These could include meeting with your team or other adults in your school to talk about this child, calling his or her parents to brainstorm ways that you can work together for the well-being of their child, or seeing yourself as an emotional coach for your student (encouraging him or her through any turbulent times).

One of the greatest gifts a teacher possesses is the opportunity to touch a child's world each day in ways that will affect that person for the rest of his or her life. We never know when a moment in time with a student will be a moment forever. I wish you all the best as you continue to be a significant adult in the lives of your students.

—David A. Levine
Accord, New York
July 2005

Appendix

This appendix offers specific practices and processes which support a culture of empathy and emotional safety. These suggestions will give you a foundation in many of the ideas presented in the body of *Teaching Empathy*. Page references in the appendix will direct you to specific ideas in the book.

Culture-Building Rituals That Promote Empathy

Rituals help create new habits of thinking and acting. When the rituals are interconnected, promoting caring and compassion, then a cultural way of empathetic thinking and acting will be felt. The following rituals are examples of cultural practices that teach empathy.

- Start each day or week with a *class meeting* for "checking in" and to practice listening to each other (page 80).

- Run a fishbowl when a pressing issue, conflict, or concern needs to be addressed (page 84).

- Have students write journal entries on a variety of real-life experiences (page 75).

- Practice moral dilemma scenarios on a regular basis (page 31).

- Read a quote or poem each morning (or once a week) to your students and spend 10 minutes exploring its meaning.

Increasing Emotional Literacy (page 62)

The most critical kind of emotional intelligence for empathy is the skill of listening. Emotional literacy requires high-level listening, which incorporates three different listening perspectives:

1. Listening to the emotions of the speaker (the true feelings).

2. Listening to the thoughts of the speaker (the opinions and reasoning).

3. Listening to the intentions of the speaker (the motivations or expectations).

Teaching Frameworks

Within the cultural dynamics of emotional safety that this resource helps to create, it is critical to teach a structured step-by-step procedure for applying the skill of empathy. I call the structured process presented here Event-Empathy-Action or EEA.

Event-Empathy-Action (EEA)

I created Event-Empathy-Action (EEA) as a three-step, advanced listening approach that teaches students how to respond to others empathically. When something unfortunate, disappointing, or sad happens in another person's life—such as a family separation, doing poorly on a test, not being invited to a party, or being embarrassed in front of others—a person using the EEA method asks him- or herself the following open-ended questions:

- What happened? *(the event)*
- How is that person feeling? (*empathy*)
- What will I do? (a specific *action*)

Initially, students are led through these questions by the teacher. The hope is that in time they will learn to naturally (or automatically) respond to others by thinking through the three questions.

The EEA method is presented to the group using *empathic situations*—hypothetical scenarios a class can discuss in order to explore various empathic responses.

Sample empathy scenarios:

- A classmate just found out that she has to move because her father was transferred.

- A new student has just arrived in school today and he is sitting alone in the cafeteria.

You can create additional empathic scenarios or brainstorm some situations with your class. Daily school events provide a rich palette of challenging social situations. For a detailed sequence of lessons to teach EEA, see part 4 of *Building Classroom Communities* (Levine, 2003).

The Four Phases of Empathy

Goldstein presents the four phases of empathy training by Keefe in the book *The Prepare Curriculum* (Goldstein, 1999, paraphrased from Keefe, 1976). Keefe's process provides a framework to consider when teaching empathy and other prosocial skills. The four phases are as follows:

1. **Perceptual:** This phase focuses on teaching the students how to effectively read a social cue such as facial or body expressions. This is best taught by teaching observational skills for the purpose of providing observational feedback.

2. **Reverberatory:** Once a person has successfully perceived that something is going on with another through their observation of social cues, he or she is able to "feel" that the other person needs support in some way. In essence the other person's place of need is reverberating or echoing back to the empathizer. This can be facilitated by asking students the question, "Who has ever felt this way?" This question helps the listener reflect on a specific episode in his or her life. This episodic reflection is

ingrained into a person's memory by having him or her attach an emotion to the episode.

3. **Cognitive and affective responses:** This phase helps the empathizer sort out the feelings which are being expressed (not necessarily through words but more so through actions). For example, if a person has a furrowed brow and raised voice in the middle of a stressful situation, the empathizer is able to reason from the social cues that the other person is angry. Once this is understood, the empathizer can decide what the best response would be for the angry person.

4. **Communication phase:** In this phase the empathizer provides feedback to the other person either through active listening or direct information. For example, the empathizer could say, "You seem really upset. Would you like to sit down and talk about it?"

Symbol Name Aim Plan: The SNAP Approach to Team Building, Consensus, and Planning

Symbol Name Action Plan (SNAP) is a student planning model which integrates strategic planning, team building, creative problem solving, and social skills practice. It was initially developed by teacher, social worker, and trainer John Eddington and is used here by permission. John presents his own version of SNAP in *First Survive, Then Thrive* (see the Additional Resources section on page 213).

SNAP uses the following steps:

Step One: Identify the Problems

Students brainstorm concerns that exist within the classroom or school. Select problems that students could help solve. Some sample concerns which students can influence include:

- There is no formal welcome for new students who move into our school during the school year.

- The orientation program for incoming sixth graders to our middle school is "lame."

- There are not enough extracurricular activities for those kids who do not like sports.

An example of a concern they do not have influence over would be their dislike of food in the cafeteria.

Step Two: Select a Problem

Once a list has been brainstormed and clarified, each student can vote for two or three problems he or she thinks are the most important. Allow students only one vote per item. A facilitator or group leader slowly reads the list and the votes are offered. This is called an "energy vote" because this voting process helps identify where the energy of the group is focused. After each person has voted, the two items with the most votes are voted on again with each person only voting once. The problem with the most votes will be the focus of the planning group or team.

Step Three: Analyze the Problem

Have the team divide a sheet of paper into two columns. On the left side, the team identifies causes of the problem. After a few causes have been offered, an effect for each cause is written on the right side next to the accompanying cause. For example, if the *problem* is that a new kid has a difficult time coming into a new school, a cause might be "no one knows the new kid" and the effect might be "no one talks to him." The next cause could be "no one talks to him" and the effect would be "he feels alone and disconnected."

Step Four: Brainstorm Solutions

Students brainstorm ideas for solutions, keeping in mind that these are ideas and not strategies. Confusing ideas with strategies is a common planning error at this point as students try to plot out the exact plan (the strategy) before having a focus (the idea). An example of a strategy offered as a solution is:

- Let's make sure we include the new kid by inviting him to eat lunch with us.

This might instead come later as a strategy for a chosen solution such as:

- Let's create a program for new students in which we
  include them in everything we do at school.

Encourage students to brainstorm unique and creative solutions which could impact the problem. After 8 to 10 solutions are offered, the facilitator reviews the list and clarifies any answers if necessary.

Step Five: Choose a Solution and Create a Symbol and Name

Students vote on the solutions by using the "energy vote" process outlined in step two. Once the solution is chosen (a student-led orientation program, for example), students are divided into groups of three or four that are assigned different tasks. A few groups will create "symbols" that represent the solution, other groups will create names that clearly express the solution, and still other groups will write slogans. This is a good time to teach the class about acronyms (such as the acronym SNAP).

When the names and slogans are created, post all of them on a blank sheet of paper. A spokesperson from each group then explains the concept or meaning behind his or her group's creation and together the class either chooses a symbol and name or (preferably) synthesizes as much of the symbols and names as possible to create a combined offering.

The synthesis process: The idea is to synthesize the concepts and not necessarily to literally combine all the symbols or names or slogans. For example, one group may have come up with *The Welcoming School,* and another may have come up with an acronym such as HALL: Helping All Listen and Learn. These two names could be combined into the Welcoming Hall of Fame.

Some symbols might show an older student shaking hands with a younger one or a bridge connecting an elementary school with the middle school. A combination would show a bridge connecting the two schools with two students standing on the bridge shaking hands with the title The Welcoming Hall of Fame with the slogan, "We Help New Kids in the Hall."

Step Six: Write the Aim Statement

The aim statement is a refined way of expressing the solution. This statement identifies the problem, who it affects, the desired outcome, and how it will be addressed. The aim statement is a template to be completed.

Here is a sample aim statement for a Welcoming Hall of Fame:

Our aim is to <u>create the Welcoming Hall of Fame</u> (the solution) to help <u>incoming students to our school</u> (target population) so <u>they will feel welcomed and comfortable</u> (the outcome). This program will <u>make our school a place where all new students can learn to their best ability</u> (the overall goal).

Step Seven: Create the Plan

After creating the symbol, name, and slogan, and writing the aim statement, students now focus on the strategy or strategies for implementing their solution. In our example, the strategies for implementing the Welcoming Hall of Fame could include:

- Doing team-building activities with the new students

- Identifying where the activities will occur

- Ensuring new students know where they can find welcoming activities

- Understanding what information will be shared to help the newcomers feel comfortable in the middle school

After the planning strategies are completed, the class organizes them into a strategy chart that "unpacks" each strategy into action steps in order for them to be completed.

Following are the headings which must be completed to make sure the plan will take place effectively:

Strategy	Steps	Who Is Responsible?	Do By
Activities to do with new kids	1. Use the book *Playfair**	Jodi	April 15
	2. Try some activities	The team	April 22
	3. Pick favorites	Gideon and Sam	April 30

**Playfair: Everybody's Guide to Noncompetitive Play* by Matt Weinstein and Joel Goodman (1980)

SNAP is an efficient planning process that acts as a team builder as the students work together to synthesize their ideas for the symbol, the names, and the slogan. They can be used to promote the program around the school on posters, T-shirts and stickers. The symbol, name, and slogan give the plan and the student group an identity.

Song Lyrics from the *Teaching Empathy* CD

Howard Gray (Lee Domann)

Most everyone I knew put the
whole Gray family down.
They were the poorest family in
that little country town.

Howard always looked too big for
his funny ragged clothes.
The kids all laughed at him and
Jimmy Jones would thumb his
nose.
Howard sat across from me in seventh grade at school.
I didn't like it much but Mama
taught the Golden Rule.

So when the spit balls flew at
him, I never would join in.
I guess that was the reason
Howard thought I was his
friend.
And after things would quiet
down, sometimes I'd turn and
see
the grateful eyes of Howard Gray
looking back at me.

Howard Gray, oh Howard Gray,
somehow they got their kicks out
of treating you that way.
Deep down, I kind of liked you,
but I was too afraid
to be a friend to you, Howard
Gray.

One day after lunch, I went to
comb my hair and saw
they had Howard pinned against
a locker in the hall.
They were poking fun about that
big hole in his shirt.
They had his left arm twisted
back behind him 'til it hurt.

To this day I can't explain and I
won't try to guess
just how it was I wound up laughing harder than the rest.
I laughed until I cried but through
my tears I still could see
the tear-stained eyes of Howard
Gray looking back at me.

Howard Gray, oh Howard Gray,
I can't believe I joined 'em all
treating you that way.
Well, I wanted to apologize but I
was too afraid
of what they'd think about me,
Howard Gray.

From that moment on after I'd
made fun of him,
he never looked my way; he
never smiled at me again.
And not much longer after that,
his family moved away
and that's the last I ever saw or
heard of Howard Gray.

Howard Gray (continued)

That was twenty years ago and I
* still haven't found*
just why we'll kick a brother or a
* sister when they're down.*
Well, I know it may sound crazy,
* but now and then I dream*
about the eyes of Howard Gray
* looking back at me.*

Howard Gray, oh Howard Gray,
I've never quite forgiven us for
* treating you that way.*
I hope that maybe somehow you
* can hear this song someday*
and you'll know that I am sorry,
* Howard Gray.*

We'll probably never meet again;
* all I can do is pray—*
may you and God forgive us,
* Howard Gray.*

Courage

By Bob Blue

A small thing once happened at
   school
that brought up a question for
   me,
and somehow it taught me to see
the price that I pay to be cool.

Diane is a girl that I know.
She's strange like she doesn't
   belong.
I don't mean to say that that's
   wrong,
we don't like to be with her
   though.

And so when we all made a plan
to have this big party at Sue's,
most kids in our school got the
   news
but no one invited Diane.

The thing about Taft Junior High
is secrets don't last very long.
I acted like nothing was wrong
when I saw Diane start to cry.

I know you may think that I'm
   cruel.
It doesn't make me very proud,
I just went along with the crowd.
It's sad but you have to in school.

You can't pick the friends you pre-
   fer
you fit in as well as you can.
I couldn't be friends with Diane
'cause then they would treat me
   like her.

In one class at Taft Junior High,
we study what people have done
with gas chamber, bomber, and
   gun
in Auschwitz, Japan, and My Lai.

I don't understand all I learn.
Sometimes I just sit there and cry.
The whole world stood idly by
to watch as the innocent burned.

Like robots obeying some rules,
atrocities done by the mob,
all innocent just doing their job,
and what was it for—was it cool?

The world was aware of these
   crimes
but nobody cried out in shame.
No heroes, and no one to blame?
A story that no one dared tell.

I promise to do all I can
to not let it happen again,
to care for all women and men.
I'll start by inviting Diane.

Let Me In

Please let me in; don't push me away.
I need you to listen to my words today.
You don't even know what I've seen or where I've been.
Please, please, will you let me in?

I don't know why you all treat me this way.
First you call me names: then you say it's just play.
I feel like I did something wrong or committed a sin.
Please, please, will you let me in?

Please let me in; don't push me away.
I need you to listen to my words today.
You don't even know what I've seen or where I've been.
Please, please, will you let me in?

Every day people are walkin' around this school.
Some are treated like stars; others like a fool.
It's time that we stop, look inside at the person within.
Why can't we just let them in?

Please let me in; don't push me away.
I need you to listen to my words today.
You don't even know what I've seen or where I've been.
Please, please let me in.

We All Have A Gift

We all have a gift,
our place in the world.
Each one helps the tribe.
There's a lot that we can do.
   (sung twice)

Like an eagle, some fly high,
soaring in the sky.
The inventor tries new things,
imagines what they'll bring.

We all have a gift,
our place in the world.
Each one helps the tribe.
There's a lot that we can do.
   (sung twice)

If ever people fight,
the deer makes things alright.
Peacemaker they shall be,
helps communicate and see.

We all have a gift,
our place in the world.
Each one helps the tribe.
There's a lot that we can do.
   (sung twice)

Everything has its place.
Bear will keep the space.
Organizer, solid friend,
you can count on them.

We all have a gift,
our place in the world.
Each one helps the tribe.
There's a lot that we can do.
   (sung twice)

When the day has come and
   gone,
buffalo gets things done;
has energy times ten,
tomorrow will do it all again.

We all have a gift,
our place in the world.
Each one helps the tribe.
There's a lot that we can do.
   (sung twice)

There's a lot that we can do.

Lift Me Up

Lift me up, don't put me down.
Lift my feet up off the ground.
If I'm lost, help me feel found.
Lift me up, don't put me down,
  down, down.
Down, down, down.
Lift me up.

Did you ever wake up and have a
  bad morning—
Didn't know if you were coming or
  going?
You need a friend to bring you
  around—
lift you up, not put you down.

Lift me up, don't put me down.
Lift my feet up off the ground.
If I'm lost, help me feel found.
Lift me up, don't put me down,
  down, down.
Down, down, down.
Lift me up.

Say in class you give the wrong
  answer,
And you're met with foolish
  laughter.
Take your laughter and get out of
  town!
Lift me up, don't put me down.

Lift me up, don't put me down.
Lift my feet up off the ground.
If I'm lost, help me feel found.
Lift me up, don't put me down,
  down, down.
Down, down, down.
Lift me up.

In the cafeteria for something to eat
But you can't find a seat.
There's a smiling face says,
  "Sit here friend."
Makes you happy once again.

Lift me up, don't put me down.
Lift my feet up off the ground.
If I'm lost, help me feel found.
Lift me up, don't put me down,
  down, down.
Down, down, down.
Lift me up.

Every day as you make your choices,
can you hear all the voices
of the people in this town
calling out a familiar sound:

Lift me up, don't put me down.
Lift my feet up off the ground.
If I'm lost, help me feel found.
Lift me up, don't put me down,
  down, down.
Down, down, down.
Lift me up.

Stop and Think

Stop and think.
Take a breath.
Check your feelings
before you act.
Stop and think,
don't hurt a friend.
Stop and think
if you get mad.

Once at lunch,
someone bumped me.
I dropped my tray.
I was steamed.
I stopped
and took a real deep breath.
Next thing I know she helped me
  out.

Stop and think.
Take a breath.
Check your feelings
before you act.
Stop and think.
Don't hurt a friend.
Stop and think
if you get mad.

When my team
lost a game.
I was angry
as could be.
My friend said, "Stop."
She smiled at me.
"Stop and think.

Just let things be."
Stop and think.
Take a breath.
Check your feelings
before you act.
Stop and think.
Don't hurt a friend.
Stop and think
if you get mad.

Every day
of your life,
you can choose
to do things right.
If you stop and think
instead of getting mad,
you'll feel better,
you won't feel sad.

Stop and think.
Take a breath.
Check your feelings
before you act.
Stop and think.
Don't hurt a friend.
Stop and think
if you get mad.

Music Credits

"Howard Gray"
David Levine, vocals and guitar
Dean Jones, drums and piano
Debbie Lan, vocals
John P. Hughes, vocals
Fooch Fischetti, pedal steel guitar
John Parker, upright bass

"Courage"
David Levine, vocals and guitars
Dean Jones, bass, drums, and percussion
Fooch Fischetti, pedal steel

"Let Me In"
David Levine, vocals, guitar, and mandolin
Dean Jones, organ, drums, bass, and percussion
Fooch Fischetti, pedal steel guitar

"We All Have a Gift"
David Levine, vocals and guitar
Dean Jones, vocals, drums, bass, and electric guitar
Debbie Lan, vocals
John P. Hughes, vocals

"Lift Me Up"
David Levine, vocals, guitar, and mandolin
Dean Jones, drums and bass
Debbie Lan, vocals
John P. Hughes, vocals

"Stop and Think"
David Levine, vocals and guitar
Dean Jones, vocals, bass, and drums
(With special thanks to my good friend Jodi Palinkas who said, "Stop and think: just let things be.")

"Mrs. Lopez (I'll Never Forget You)"
David Levine, vocals and guitar
Jay Ungar, fiddle
Molly Mason, bass

All songs © 2005 by David A. Levine, Swinging Door Music (BMI) except "Mrs. Lopez" © 1992

"Howard Gray" © 1985 by Lee Domann, Shuretone Music (BMI) and Renovation Music (BMI)
Used with permission.

"Courage" © 1988 by Bob Blue, Black Socks Music (www.the-spa.com/bobblue1/)
Used with permission.

Produced by David A. Levine and Dean Jones

All songs recorded and mixed by Dean Jones at No Parking Studios, Rosendale, New York, except "Mrs. Lopez (I'll Never Forget You)," the introduction to "Howard Gray," and the spoken lyrics to "Howard Gray" and "Courage," which were recorded by Chris Andersen at Nevessa Production, Woodstock.

Mastered by Chris Andersen at Nevessa

Additional Resources

Cajete, G. (1994). *Look to the mountain: An ecology of indigenous education.* Durango, CO: Kivaki Press.

Cohen, J. (Ed.). (1999). *Educating minds and hearts: Social emotional learning and the passage into adolescence.* New York: Teachers College Press.

Curwin, R. (1992). *Rediscovering hope: Our greatest teaching strategy.* Bloomington, IN: Solution Tree Press (formerly National Educational Service).

DePaola, T. (1988). *The legend of the Indian paintbrush.* New York: Putnam.

Eddington, J., & Rosato, B. (1998). *First survive, then thrive: The journey from crisis to transformation.* Tempe, AZ: American Federation of Astrologers.

Goleman, D. (1995). *Emotional intelligence: Why it can matter more than IQ.* New York: Bantam Books.

Kavasch, E. B. (1999). *Apache children and their elders talk together.* New York: PowerKids Press. (Kavasch has written a number of books in this series, including books on the Blackfoot, Lakota Sioux, and Seminole tribes.)

Kriete, R. (2002). *The morning meeting book.* Greenfield, MA: The Northeast Foundation for Children.

Lantieri, L. (2001). *Schools with spirit: Nurturing the inner lives of children and teachers.* Boston: Beacon Press.

Levine, D. A. (Writer/Producer). (1996). *Through the eyes of Howard Gray* [Video program]. Accord, New York: Blue Heron Press.

Mahdi, L., Christopher, N., & Meade, M. (Eds.). (1996). *Crossroads: The quest for contemporary rites of passage.* Chicago: Open Court Publishing.

Marshall, J., III. (2001). *The Lakota way: Stories and lessons for living, Native American wisdom on ethics and character.* New York: Penguin Compass.

Moorman, C. (2001). *Spirit whisperers: Teachers who nourish a child's spirit.* Merrill, MI: Personal Power Press.

Nye, N. (1992). *This same sky: A collection of poems from around the world.* New York: Four Winds Press.

Nye, N. S. (1998). *The space between our footsteps: Poems and paintings from the Middle East.* New York: Simon and Schuster.

Schniedewind, N., & Davidson, E. (1987). *Cooperative learning, cooperative lives: A sourcebook of learning activities for building a peaceful world.* Dubuque, IA: William C. Brown.

Smith, D. W., (1989). *The circle of acquaintance: Perception, consciousness, and empathy.* Dordrecht, Holland, and Boston: Kluwer Academic Publishers.

Somé, M. P. (1993). *Ritual: Power, healing, and community.* Portland, OR: Swan/Raven & Company.

Wlodkowski, R. J., & Ginsburg, M. B. (1995). *Diversity and motivation: Culturally responsive teaching.* San Francisco: Jossey-Bass.

References

Add Health: The National Longitudinal Study of Adolescent Health (n.d.). Retrieved July 29, 2005, from University of North Carolina at Chapel Hill, Carolina Population Center web site: www.cpc.unc.edu/projects/addhealth.

Atlas, R. S., & Pepler, D. J. (1998). Observations of bullying in the classroom. *The Journal of Educational Research, 92,* 86–97.

Bandura, A. (1997). *Self-efficacy: The Exercise of Control.* New York: W. H. Freeman and Company.

Beck, P.V., Walters, A. L., & Francisco, N. (1977). *The Sacred: Ways of knowledge, sources of life.* Tsaile, AZ: Navajo Community College Press.

Brendtro, L. K., & Seita, J. R. (2004). *Kids who outwit adults.* Bloomington, IN: Solution Tree Press (formerly National Educational Service).

Brendtro, L., Brokenleg, M., & Van Bockern, S. (2002). *Reclaiming youth at risk: Our hope for the future.* Bloomington, IN: Solution Tree Press (formerly National Educational Service).

Brokenleg, M. (1998). Native wisdom and belonging. *Reclaiming Children and Youth, 7*(3), 130–133.

Coltrane, J. (1966). Liner notes of *Meditations.* Interview by Nat Hentoff. New York: MCA Records/Impulse.

Cooper, R. K., & Sawaf, A. (1997). *Executive EQ: Emotional intelligence in leadership and organizations.* New York: Grosset/Putnam.

Covey, S. R. (2004). *The 7 habits of highly effective people: Powerful lessons in personal change.* New York: Free Press.

Day, L. (2001). *The circle: How the power of a single wish can change your life.* New York: Jeremy P. Tarcher/Putnam.

DuFour, R., & Eaker, R. (1998). *Professional learning communities at work: Best practices for enhancing student achievement.* Bloomington, IN: Solution Tree Press (formerly National Educational Service).

Franke, R. (1983). For real. On *For Real* [CD]. Cambridge, MA: Flying Fish and Rounder Records.

Frost, R. (1920). *Mountain Interval.* New York: Henry Holt and Company. Bartleby.com, 1999, www.bartleby.com/119/.

Fulghum, R. (1988). *All I really need to know I learned in kindergarten: Uncommon thoughts on common things.* New York: Villard Books.

Gandhi, A. (2003). *Legacy of love: My education in the path of nonviolence.* Sobrante, CA: North Bay Books, p. 137. (Citation provided by the Gandhi Institute, www.gandhiinstitute.org.)

Garbarino, J. (1999). *Lost boys: Why our sons turn violent and how we can save them.* New York: Free Press.

Garbarino, J., & deLara, E. (2002). *And words can hurt forever: How to protect adolescents from bullying, harassment, and emotional violence.* New York: Free Press.

Gladwell, M. (2000). *The tipping point: How little things can make a big difference.* Boston: Little, Brown.

Goldstein, A. P. (1999). *The prepare curriculum: Teaching prosocial competencies.* Champaign, IL: Research Press.

Goleman, D. (1998). *Working with emotional intelligence.* New York: Bantam Books.

Goleman, D., Boyatzis, R., & McKee, A. (2002). *Primal leadership: Learning to lead with emotional intelligence.* Boston, MA: Harvard Business School Press.

Greenleaf, R. (1998). *The power of two.* Newfield, ME: Greenleaf Learning.

Hoover, J. H., & Olsen, G. W. (2001). *Teasing and harassment: The frames and scripts approach for teachers and parents.* Bloomington, IN: Solution Tree Press (formerly National Educational Service).

Keefe, T. (1976). Empathy: The critical skill. *Social Work, 21*(1), 10–14.

Kohlberg, L., Lieberman, M., Higgins, A., & Power, C. (1981). The just community school and its curriculum: Implications for the future. *Moral Education Forum, 6*(4), 31–42.

Levine, D. A. (2003). *Building classroom communities: Strategies for developing a culture of caring.* Bloomington, IN: Solution Tree Press (formerly National Educational Service).

Marano, H. E. (1996, December 25). Teachers as bullies: Norwegian's study finds "dirty secret." *The New York Times,* p. C6.

Maslow, A. H. (1993). *The farther reaches of human nature.* New York: Penguin.

Nye, N. S. (1998). *The space between our footsteps: Poems and paintings from the Middle East.* New York: Simon and Schuster.

O'Donohue, J. (2005). Retrieved January 15, 2005, from the John O'Donohue web site: www.jodonohue.com.

Plotkin, B. (1999). *Training intensive: Soulcraft journey,* Durango, CO. Animus Valley Institute.

Plotkin, B. (2003). *Soulcraft: Crossing into the mysteries of nature and psyche.* Novato, CA: New World Library.

Resnick, M. D., Bearman, P. S., Blum, R. W., Bauman, K. E., Harris, K. M., Jones, J., Tabor, J., Beuhring, T., Sieving, R. E., Shew, M., Ireland, M., Bearinger, L. H., & Udry, J. R. (1997). Protecting adolescents from harm: Findings from the National Longitudinal Study on Adolescent Health. *The Journal of the American Medical Association, 278*(10), 823-832.

Sarton, M. (1971). The invocation to Kali. In *A grain of mustard seed.* New York: W. W. Norton.

Senge, P., Kleiner, A., Roberts, C., Ross, R., & Smith, B. (1994). *The fifth discipline fieldbook.* New York: Currency, Doubleday.

Sergiovanni, T. J. (2004). Building a community of hope. *Educational Leadership, 61*(8), 33–37.

Schaps, E. (May 2, 2002). Speech given at the Assets-Based Character Education Conference in Meriden, Connecticut.

Storm, H. (1972). *Seven arrows.* New York: Harper and Row.

Stossel, J. (Writer). (2002). *The "in" crowd: Competition among kids, competition to belong is fierce* [Television serial episode of "20/20"]. New York: ABC Television.

Tuckman, B. (1965). Developmental sequence in small groups. *Psychological bulletin, 63,* 384–399.

Turney, T. (1994). *Peer leadership: A human relations process to reduce substance abuse and improve school climate.* Mountainside, NJ: Turney Publishing.

Weinstein, M., & Goodman, J. (1980). *Playfair: Everybody's guide to noncompetitive play.* San Luis Obispo, CA: Impact Publishers.

Whyte, D. (1997). *The house of belonging.* Langley, WA: Many Rivers Press.

Whyte, D. (2001). *Crossing the unknown sea: Work as a pilgrimage of identity.* New York: Riverhead Books.

Whyte, D. (August 10, 2001). Through the eye of the needle: Life, work, and the poetic imagination. Workshop presentation in Esopus, New York.

Williamson, M. (1997). *Being in light: Lectures based on a course in miracles* [4-tape set]. Carlsbad, CA: Hay House.

Williamson, M. (2002). *Everyday grace: Having hope, finding forgiveness, and making miracles.* New York: Riverhead Books.

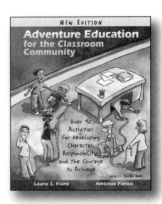

Adventure Education for the Classroom Community: Over 90 Activities for Developing Character, Responsibility, and the Courage to Achieve
Laurie S. Frank and Ambrose Panico
New edition! Engaging activities encourage your students to create a classroom community that supports character development, academic excellence, and individual and social responsibility. **BKF221**

Building Classroom Communities: Strategies for Developing a Culture of Caring
David A. Levine
This resource will help you create a unified, caring classroom in which all students feel they belong and love the learning process. **BKF145**

The Bullying Prevention Handbook: A Guide for Principals, Teachers, and Counselors
John H. Hoover and Ronald L. Oliver
Second Edition! Solve bully-victim problems through education, mediation, and cultivation of respect and caring. New chapters explore modern-day issues like cyberbullying, "gay bashing," and more. **BKF233**

The School of Belonging Plan Book
David A. Levine
This plan book helps you build a culture of caring where students feel safe and are nurtured toward achievement. **BKF218**

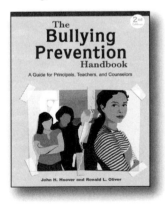